SAC ... RY
S ...
D0172100
...009

Zombies

A Field Guide to the Walking Dead

Zombies

A Field Guide to the Walking Dead

By Dr. Bob Curran

Illustrated by Ian Daniels

New Page Books

A Division of The Career Press, Inc.

Copyright © 2009 by Bob Curran

All rights reserved under the Pan-American and International Copyright Conventions. This book may not be reproduced, in whole or in part, in any form or by any means electronic or mechanical, including photocopying, recording, or by any information storage and retrieval system now known or hereafter invented, without written permission from the publisher, The Career Press.

Zombies

Edited and Typeset by Gina Talucci

Designed by Lu Rossman/Digi Dog Design NYC

Cover and interior art by Ian Daniels

Printed in the U.S.A. by Book-mart Press

To order this title, please call toll-free 1-800-CAREER-1 (NJ and Canada: 201-848-0310) to order using VISA or MasterCard, or for further information on books from Career Press.

CAREER PRESS

New Page BOOKS

The Career Press, Inc., 3 Tice Road, PO Box 687,
Franklin Lakes, NJ 07417

www.careerpress.com
www.newpagebooks.com

Library of Congress Cataloging-in-Publication Data

Curran, Bob.

Zombies : a field guide to the walking dead / by Bob Curran.

p. cm.

Includes bibliographical reference and index.

ISBN 978-1-60163-022-3

1. Zombies. I. Title.

GR581.C87 2009

398.21—dc22

2008020791

Contents

Introduction

Out of the Tomb

The jaw is slack with a small trace of dribbling saliva about the lips, the eyes are glazed, and on the bone the skin is desiccated, rotting, and withered; the footstep are shambling and hesitant. The creature lurches from side to side as it moves, perhaps not truly under its own volition, but certainly with some sort of dreadful purpose. Its movements are sharp and jerky, similar to those of an automaton directed by some power outside itself. It moves relentlessly forward, craving living human flesh.

This is perhaps the representation of the walking dead—the zombie—with which we are all most familiar. It has appeared on both film and

The Zombie

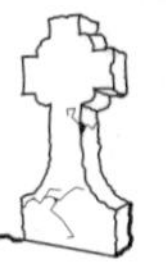

television screens so often—in films such as George A. Romero's *Night of the Living Dead* or the cartoon antics of Scooby Doo on *Zombie Island,* for example—that it has become almost ingrained into our psyche. But is this image an accurate one? Does it truly reflect what we believe the walking dead to be, or is it merely a reflection of a kind of cinematic belief—something that looks eerie and menacing on the big screen? And is the cultural perception of the risen dead a wider one than the slack-jawed zombie of celluloid fame?

Since earliest times, the return of the dead from beyond the grave has always been somewhat problematic. Some would no doubt welcome the return of their loved ones who have passed away; others might fear it. Some might welcome the dead back from the tomb; others might recoil from the returning cadavers. In some instances, the returning dead might signal good luck for a household; in others it might threaten immense and immediate danger. Other households take the return of a loved one from beyond the grave almost as a matter of course.

Strange Tales From Different Times

In 1993, my wife and I interviewed an old man, living in Wheathill (south-western County Fermanagh in the north of Ireland). He was a well-respected figure in his community and a leader in the local church, but despite these things he told a strange story. As a boy, almost 80 years prior, he remembered his grandfather, who had been dead for less than a year, coming back to the house to sit at the fire and enjoy a pipe of tobacco, just as he had done in life. This had occurred at Halloween, when the dead were traditionally expected to return.

"He just lifted the latch of the door and came in," the old man informed me, "but we had his pipe ready for him." He also had a glass of whiskey in order to "warm him after nearly a year in the clay," and sometimes even a meal (apparently he ate just as heartily as any living person). The old man remembered climbing on grandfather's knee, but feeling the touch of his skin to be "very cold."

"Were you not frightened?" I asked him. He shook his head.

"Why would I be?" he replied. "It was my own grandfather." The only difference that he noticed was that the returning cadaver could not speak. He could, however, communicate by gesture and by facial expression, but very few members of the family seemed to speak to him. He simply sat and enjoyed the goings on around him—the bustle of his relatives and descendants—just as he would have done if alive.

As the evening drew to a close, the family retired to bed, leaving him sitting in front of the fire, smoking his pipe contentedly. When they came down the following morning, he had gone back to the tomb. No real fuss was made; it was just as if a favored relative had been visiting them.

Later, I spoke to the old man's sister who, without any collaboration or prompting, described the event just as he had told it. The cadaver had returned only once as far as she could remember, but she too remembered seeing it. (She lived close by, but had not been present when the story was related. Moreover, we went straight from the old man's house to hers.) After that, perhaps her grandfather's body had been too decomposed for him to return.

A committed Christian, the old man firmly believed that on certain nights of the year, such as Halloween, God briefly permitted the dead to return to bring comfort to their loved ones and provide a reassurance of the Afterlife. Such corpses could only return, he was sure, with God's permission.

My wife suggested that he and his sister might be playing some sort of joke on us, but, as I said, why should they? Both were respected elderly members of the community, both were well connected in the local church, both were extremely serious when they told the story, and what did they stand to gain by telling it? I, myself, felt inclined to believe them, but I come from traditions that believe the dead might return.

Growing up in an extremely rural and isolated region of the Mourne Mountains in County Down, I was well aware of the strong perception that death was simply not the end, and that those who lay in local churchyards might, from time to time, return to the houses in which they'd once lived to be among their families once more. Whether or not such a return was wholly welcomed is another matter, but it was treated as a fact. On Halloween night several families set an extra place at the supper table in case a dead relative would turn up unexpectedly. One old lady, who lived not very far from us, spread gleeshins (fine dust and residue) from the fire out on her hearthstone before she went to bed on Halloween night. If they were disturbed in the morning, she knew that her dead ancestors had been there the previous evening, and had danced in front of the fireplace as they had done in times past. She would also leave a piece of cake and a glass of whiskey by the fire in case the dead would be hungry when they gathered there—in very much the same way as we children left something for Santa Claus. I have no idea as to whether these items were consumed or not, but there were yet other instances of the returning dead.

The returning dead in these instances were more or less welcomed, but there were others who seemed to rise from the grave with a more malignant purpose. On the edge of the Sperrin Mountains in County Tyrone, a man showed me a coat that he claimed had been torn by the hands of the dead one night as he unadvisedly crossed a graveyard on his way home. Had the material of the coat not given, he assured me, the dead would have torn him limb from limb. The dead hated the living and were always trying to do them harm, he continued. Of course, it might be possible to argue that he had caught his coat on a briar or a low branch as he darted across the cemetery, but he was in no doubt that it had been the clutch of the waking dead, stirred in their graves by his presence above them.

In the same part of County Fermanagh in which I had interviewed the old man, I heard another story. In Arny, near the Cavan-Fermanagh border, another woman died in childbirth, but the child lived and was once again raised by the father. However, each night, the woman would return from the grave and attempt to steal the infant away, and take it back with her to the tomb. The distraught husband used a number of devices to divert the cadaver, including feeding it cheese (which was the woman's favorite food when she was alive), but eventually he had to place a holy protection on the crib in order to keep the cadaver away. At this the woman stayed in her grave and troubled her house no more; the child was safe. A blind fiddler living near the village of Blacklion in County Cavan told this legend to me. The fiddler named several people who could actually verify it, including a descendant of the child. Some of the returning corpses, therefore, were not terribly friendly toward the living, and might return to the world in order to fulfil to their own dark agendas.

None of these dead were the insubstantial, vaguely transparent "ghosts" that passed easily and blithely through walls and doors, which were the legacies of the Victorian era. Rather, these were substantial and solid cadavers that behaved in the same ways that living people did. They could eat a meal, get drunk, perform conjugal rights, fight, and even kill people if they so chose. They could be violent if crossed, for they often had the same emotions as the

living, such as love, hate, envy, and so on. They might also carry out tasks that they had left unfinished in life. A well-known story from Cork in the Irish Republic tells of Grace Connor, a seamstress who had been paid to make a wedding dress for a bride, but who died before the job could be completed. Each night she returned from the tomb in order to complete the stitching, working by candlelight to finish the dress that was ready for the wedding day as promised. There are similar stories from the west off Scotland and from many parts of England and Cornwall as well.

Grace Connor

Such beliefs confined are not solely to Western Europe, however. From Romania, for example, Professor Harry Senn recounts a story in his *The Werewolf and Vampire in Eastern Europe* concerning a traveler who lodged for a night in a rural farmhouse. While he was having a meal with the family, the door opened, and a stranger came in and sat down at a vacant place at the table. He was served a meal along the others, which he consumed. The traveler noticed that the stranger did not speak, though the other members of the family around the table seemed to know him. As each man got up and went back to the fields, he touched the stranger on the shoulder. Eventually the man himself got up and left without a greeting or a word of thanks. The mysterious man was said to have been one of the *moroii,* the walking dead of Romania, and a former member of the family with whom he was eating. The touching of him on the shoulder was done in order to bring good luck to the household. The moroii were therefore symbols of well being and good fortune for the living. Set against this in Romanian folklore, however, are the *strigoii,* the evil walking dead who seek to use every opportunity to bring the living harm. These creatures might supernaturally enter houses to violently attack sleepers, causing them injury, and they also went about spreading disease in local communities. They were the template for the idea of the vampire, common in many Eastern European countries and further afield. And there are examples, too, from other cultures where hostile and vicious cadavers return from the grave with the sole purpose of tormenting the living. The idea of dangerous and ambulant corpses is something of a cross-cultural phenomenon.

And there was a religious element to the return of the dead as well. This was tied in with the worship of ancestors, which, arguably, is one of the oldest types of religion there is. In many cultures, the dead were both venerated and

looked upon for wisdom and protection. The great men of yore who had proved themselves particularly strong, brave, or possessed of great learning and foresight were often invoked by communities, long after their demise, hoping for their supernatural aid. Perhaps some element of this belief lies at the very roots of a belief in vampires and in zombies. In the latter, it is said, an entire religion—voodoo—has been partly built around such beliefs, as is reputedly the case with many Afro-Caribbean faiths. But it is not just in the Caribbean that such ideas flourish; other peoples around the world, in India, Japan, Tibet, and even in the early days of the Americas, all have looked to the dead and to those who have gone before. Maybe such an idea gives them a sense of continuity, and sanctions immortality and permanence in a rapidly changing and shifting world. It also gives them a sense of security against the worst that life can throw at them.

The concept of the walking dead is therefore a much more complex ideal than the celluloid ambling and slack-jawed zombie would seem to suggest. There are, for instance, both the friendly dead (those who were permitted by God to return to the existence that they had previously enjoyed before their demise, and to bring comfort to their families and descendants) and the hostile dead (those who rose from the tomb with some malignant purpose). There is also the religious element to be considered as well—those who might return to protect and advise their descendants or their communities.

But where do the origins of these beliefs lie and how have they been interpreted by the cultures in which they appear? *Zombies* seeks to explore how notions of the returning cadavers have come about and the traditions that they have evoked in the human mind. So, take a walk with us now down the dark pathways that are frequented by the ambulant dead in search of some answers. You'll be in good company!

Back From the Beyond

Resurrection, the corporeal return of the body from the grave or from some realm beyond Death, is almost as old as time itself. The origins of the walking dead may lie in ancient mythologies dating far back into the past, describing the return of either gods or great men from the Afterlife. Indeed, if we look at the legends of a number of ancient cultures we find similar tales where such entities are either brought back or return on their own terms.

Today, a vast number of philosophies and religions maintain that when we die it completely marks the end of our involvement in the living world. No matter what Afterlife we imagine for ourselves, it usually marks the end of contact with all that we know and with those whom we know. The grave—however we conceive it—is our final resting place, and from it we cannot return.

Life After Death

In many respects, the world of the living and the dead were often kept separate in many ancient cultures. In Greek thought, for example, once the soul of an individual crossed the River Styx (one of three major rivers in the Underworld), he or she was not supposed to be able to return to his or her former life or to the living world. In some cultures, such as Roman and Greek, as soon as they crossed the River Lethe (another of the Underworld rivers and the one from which we get the word *lethargic*) and inhaled its vapors, they would forget their previous existence and live in the caverns of the Underworld for eternity, totally unaware of the living world, and all connections with it completely severed.

Greece

And yet in a number of other ancient beliefs, this separation was not always so clear-cut. Indeed, in some aspects of Greek myth, death was not an absolute certainty. A persistent story dating from the time of the Roman writer Virgil, for instance, tells the story of Orpheus, a celebrated musician and monarch of the Greek kingdom of Thrace, who ventured into the Underworld in order to bring back his wife, Eurydice, from the dead. It was said that, while fleeing from the unwelcome attentions of Aristeaus, son of Apollo, Eurydice

River Lethe

(her name is sometimes given as Agriope) fell into a pit of venomous snakes, several of which bit her and killed her. Beside himself with grief, Orpheus who besides being a superb musician was also well skilled in the magical arts, resolved to travel into the land of the dead and bring her back to the world of the living. This he did, appearing in the dreadful Underworld court of Hades,

Eurydice

king of the dead, and his wife, Persephone. In that terrible court, Orpheus played his lyre so sweetly that he charmed the heart of the awful king, and Hades agreed to let Eurydice go. There was one condition, however: Orpheus must walk ahead of her all the way to the living world and must not look back—if he did so, she would be lost to him and to the living forever. Orpheus led her out of the dark Underworld and toward the light, but he forgot the condition imposed upon him and stole a brief glance backward to make sure that she was following him. At this, Eurydice returned to the dark and to death forever.

This celebrated legend, which has become a classical Greek story, may have been indicative of a belief that was reasonably common in the ancient world: It might be possible to return (or to fetch relatives or loved ones back), from the dead in a corporeal state. The dead person might then continue to enjoy life as he or she had done before, death being only a minor interruption and inconvenience. In fact, a number of cultures believed that death was simply a transition from one form of living to another, and that the dead frequently noticed little difference between the living world and the Afterlife.

Egypt

The ancient Egyptians, for example, believed that death was but a stage to another phase of existence, which was not all that different from our physical reality. This Afterlife lay in a land far away to the West. Consequently, great Pharaohs were buried with their treasures, so that they would be wealthy in this other existence; their favorite animals, so that they would continue to enjoy their company beyond Death; and their servants, who would continue to serve them in the Afterlife when the sun rose. Their bodies were preserved through a process of mummification, so that they would be whole and vigorous in the Afterlife. But once they had survived the transition from one phase to the other, there seems to have been no way back to the world of the living, in corporeal form at least, for the common Egyptian soul. Perhaps they did not wish to come back.

And yet Egyptian mythology—the ideas of gods and goddesses—is riddled with tales of return from the grave and resurrection. In Egyptian belief, even the act of transition from one world into the other through death involved a descent into the Underworld (and for the Egyptians, it was literally a journey into a subterranean world) and a reemergence, which was still in a corporeal form, just in a new existence. Some of the gods themselves had returned from the jaws of death in physical form.

Indeed one of the oldest gods in the Egyptian pantheon, Osiris, had been resurrected in such a fashion. The earliest reference to this god—who ultimately judged those who had died to see if they were fit for the Afterlife—comes from a group of writings known as the *Pyramid Texts*, which date from around 2400 BCE, when his cult was already well established along the Nile. In fact, the cult continued (as a mystery cult) for many centuries until its suppression during the Christian era.

According to the tradition, Osiris was one of the sons of Geb, an old earth god who mated with Nut, the sky goddess; he was considered to be the god of fertility. In legend, Osiris was tricked by his brother Set (considered to be an evil spirit) to climb into a coffin, which Set then immediately sealed and threw into the River Nile. This casket was subsequently found, trapped in some reeds, by the goddess Isis, who was Osiris's sister and wife. By this time Osiris was already dead, but Isis was not undaunted, for she knew a spell that

would surely bring Osiris back to life, if only briefly. This she did, with one specific purpose: so that he might impregnate her. In other variants of the story—thought to be even older—Set tore up Osiris's body and scattered it across Egypt. Isis patiently sought after the fragments and placed them together, except for the genitals, which she could not find (Set dumped them in the River Nile). Isis therefore fashioned herself a penis out of clay, which she attached to the body before reviving it, allowing Osiris to impregnate her. She would later give birth to their son Horus, the Egyptian sun god. (In a conflicting and perhaps much later myth, Horus is identified as the sun of Hathor or Nut and brother of Isis). After this act, Osiris returned once again to the grave. In drawings contained within the *Pyramid Texts,* Osiris is portrayed as a green-skinned ruler or Pharaoh, with a crook and a flail, which were the symbols of office, suggesting that Egyptian Pharaohs were descended from him, and that they, too, might have the power to return from the dead (the land in the West) if they so chose. This conferred a kind of immortality concerning the Egyptian kings, who were considered to be the embodiment of Osiris, or his counterparts Horus or Ra (another manifestation of the sun god), and therefore had power over life and death.

Frankenstein

As a passing issue, it is also interesting to note that the story concerning Isis, in which she hunts for the pieces of Osiris's body and assembles them into a whole, has resonance in the story of Mary Shelley's *Frankenstein.* Here the dubious protagonist, Victor Frankenstein, searches around for the remnants of dead corpses in order to return them into a form of life by way of his completed "monster" using elemental power (in this case electricity from lightning). It has been argued that Mary Shelley based her central character on the enigmatic and mysterious theologian and alchemist Johann Konrad Dippel (1673–1734), who was said to have inhabited Castle Frankenstein (the name *Frankenstein* simply means "Rock of the Franks") near Darmstadt in Hesse, Germany. Dippel was supposed to have engaged in macabre experiments within the fortress—including the creation of "Dippel's Oil," which was supposed to be a constituent of the elixir vitae, or, the oil of immortality, the

Frankenstein

Elixir of Life). Similar to Isis and Frankenstein, he was supposed to gather up fragments of corpses to create life using his elixir, and was reputedly driven from his castle by angry and terrified locals. Although many have argued that Dippel is the original template for Frankenstein through his creation of an animated "monster" from the remnants of the dead, the idea is much older—perhaps stretching back as far as Isis's assemblage and reanimation of Osiris.

Of course, the Egyptian idea of the death and resurrection of Osiris may have had its origins in the death and reflowering of the vegetation along the Nile, coupled with the river's flooding and subsequent recession. The notion of returning from the grave in both visible and corporeal form was not a new one, even in ancient Egypt, and was closely linked into the cycle of the year and with dying and returning growth. Nor were the Egyptians the only ancient culture to believe that their deities returned from the Underworld.

Babylonian Myth

In Babylonian and northern Semitic mythology, there were similar associations with the god Tammuz. In his original incarnation, Tammuz may well have been little more than a localized Assyrian fertility god who disappeared into the Underworld for part of the year (the onset of winter), to return in the spring. This journey was probably nothing more than a symbol of the turning year. Gradually, however, a more complex mythology built up around him, connecting him with other deities, most notably the goddess Inanna (Sumerian texts) or Ishtar (Akkadian texts). In latter texts, Tammuz also changes his name to the Sumerian Dumuzid, the shepherd-king. However, much of his tale concerns the goddess Inanna, and appears in both Sumerian and Akkadian mythology, albeit in slightly different versions. The oldest version may originate from around 2500 BCE.

For some unspecified reason Inanna made a descent into the Babylonian Underworld. This is a lightless and cheerless place known as Kur, which was inhabited by heroes, nobles, and commoners alike. According to tradition, the nobles and heroes sat in dark and gloomy caves where common people waited on them. Why Inanna should have wished to venture there is unclear; in some variations, she had been summoned there by a consortium of Underworld gods called the Anunnaki (meaning "a host of demons"), who were associated with magic and sorcery—although what their purpose was in doing so is mysterious.

There is a suggestion that they intended to take her prisoner as soon as she appeared before them, and hold her in the Underworld forever. Fearful and suspicious, Inanna instructed her servant to petition some of the other gods for their help and support. This her servant did, but only one god named Enka (also known as Ea) responded. Here the Sumerian and Akkadian texts vary slightly. However, through the magic of Enka, Inanna was restored to life with the understanding that she would find someone to take her place in Kur.

When she returned to her own country, accompanied by the servants of the Anunnaki, she found Tammuz occupying her throne and ruling as the monarch. It was Tammuz that she attacked and eventually consigned to Kur, although later he would rise again in some form, which is not specified. In an apparently older version of the tale (perhaps even pre-dating 2500 BCE) Inanna journeyed to Kur in order to retrieve Tammuz, who had been killed. To obtain his return to the world of the living, she had to stand before the Anunnaki—who in this version appear in the role of Underworld judges or assessors—to plead for his release from the world of the dead. Aided by the magic of Ea,

she succeeded and returned with Tammuz to the living world, where he reigned as Dumuzid, the shepherd-king. He was equated with a couple of legendary kings: Dumuzid of Bad-Tibera (a Sumerian city-state), who was the fifth king who ruled before the Great Flood; and Dumuzid the Fisherman, who was counted as the third king during the first dynasty of Uruk. Both of these men, according to legend, were said to be extremely powerful prehistoric kings with supernatural connotations, which, perhaps, included returning from the dead. There is also a king by the name of Dumuzid mentioned in the ancient Sangam literature of the Tamils as ruling Pandan, one of three Tamil kingdoms that existed on the southern coast of India from prehistoric times until the end of the 15th century. According to tradition, around 1750 BCE, part of the kingdom was destroyed by a great flood, and at this time Dumuzid (Tammuz) seems to have been king. It is the Sumerian king, however, who seems to have been most important, and who may have conquered death.

Indeed so important was Tammuz in the early Middle Eastern consciousness that a certain time of year was named after him, celebrating his descent into Kur. This period was not only observed by the Babylonians, but also by some of the northern Semites as well. Beginning at the start of the summer solstice, when the fierce heat began to decline and the days grew shorter, the festival of mourning the death of Tammuz lasted for approximately six days and was something of a spectacular event.

Such ritual mourning was even practiced by the strict Hebrews at the gate to the temple in Jerusalem, much to the horrified outrage of the prophet Ezekiel: "Then he brought me to the door of the gate of the Lord's house which was towards the north and behold there were women weeping for Tammuz. Then he said to me 'Hast thou seen this O son of man? Turn thee yet again and thou shalt see greater abominations than these." (Ezekiel 8:14–15)

This, along with a number of other accounts, seems to suggest that the cult of Tammuz was quite widespread amongst the early Semitic peoples. It was probably a resurrection cult because the return of Tammuz from Kur, following his victory over death, was also a cause for celebration, signaling new growth and new life. The story of Tammuz was translated from the original Babylonian by scholars Noah Kraimer and Diane Wolkstein in 1983, and may be one of a number of early resurrection texts that showed a belief in the returning and corporeal dead in ancient cultures.

The story of Tammuz/Dumuzid's resurrection has an almost exact parallel in the ancient Chola culture, which is even further East. Indeed, the returning figure that vanquishes death is also known as Dumuzid, and is named as a Chola king.

The Cholas

The Cholas, a Tamil civilization, were one (and probably one of the most influential) of a number of cultures that characterized the southern part of the Indian subcontinent and display a striking similarity with the ancient cultures of the Middle East—particularly Babylonian and Sumerian. This was probably because of trading links between the Chola and Pandan empires in Sri Lanka, southern India, and the Middle East. The legend of Tammuz is almost identical to the story told in the Middle East. Here Tammuz/Dumuzid also descends into the Underworld at the command of the gods, but he is rescued and returns to the world of the living as "a whole man" to reign for many years. He is thought to have been one of the earliest kings who ruled after a great flood (comparable to that mentioned in the Bible) had also devastated the greater part of the Chola Empire. This corresponds roughly to the Sumerian belief that Tammuz/Dumuzid was the "fifth king to rule after the Great Flood had destroyed the world."

The Middle East

Tammuz/Dumuzid was not the only ancient figure to come back from the dead in Middle Eastern belief; there was also the cult of the resurrected Ba'al. The name *Ba'al* is a complex one in ancient Middle Eastern religious examination, as the figure takes on a number of guises and is found in a number of different cultures. In each culture, the name *Ba'al* seems to have revealed a slightly different aspect. The name itself seems to be of northwest Semitic origin and simply means "lord" or "master." It could therefore have been applied to any god or supernatural being, or even to human officials. Indeed, it was interchangeable with the names of other gods from the Semitic areas such as Hadad, a northwestern Semitic storm god. Hadad was also the god of rain, fertility, and growing crops, and at one period, the two names were practically interchangeable, thus making Ba'al a fertility god. It was believed that the name *Hadad* could only be spoken by the temple priests, so the common populace therefore used the name Ba'al to describe their god or to invoke him.

To complicate matters even further, Ba'al was also a figure in the Phoenician trinity in the city of Tyre, where the name was sometimes transposed for Melqart, the son of El. Confusingly, it is thought that the name Melqart was a variation of the god Mot (an early Semitic god—also a son of El) who was the brother of Ba'al and the god of the Underworld and death. Conversely, he was also a god of vegetation and a protector of the city of Tyre itself. The Phoenicians were sea-going traders who came from a thin strip of land bordered by the Mediterranean Sea and Lebanon. They seem to have adopted some of the beliefs of other cultures, presumably to help them in their mercantile ventures, and Ba'al may have been one of them. Thus, Ba'al appears in many forms throughout the Phoenician influenced world and may have actually begun as a localized god worshipped by people with whom they traded. The

Ba'al of Lebanon, for instance, may also be Cid, "the hunter" worshipped by tribes in the north of Lebanon; Ba'al also appears as a moon god, which may be Hannon, a Semite god. One of these incarnations, however, involved resurrection and bodily return from the dead.

Ugartic Legend

Ugartic was a type of literature that emerged from the Mediterranean region, and it had roots in Sumerian and Akadian texts. In an ancient Ugardic legend, Ba'al was lured into a trap, consumed by his brother Mot, and consigned to the Underworld. Mot scattered his remains across the Middle Eastern world—a similar fate to that of Osiris in early Egyptian myth. Ba'al's sister and wife, Anat, however, ventured across the ancient world with the aid of the sun-goddess Shapesh ("the torch of the gods") gathering up the pieces and putting them together again for burial. However, she missed Ba'al and pleaded with Mot to relinquish his hold on her beloved and restore him to life, a plea that the god refused. Even El, Ba'al's father, mourned the loss of his son and "turned his face away"; as a consequence, the earth was cracked with a mighty drought. In the end, Anat lost her temper with Mot and attacked him, cleaving him in two with a sword and burning his remains. Ba'al was restored to life and continued to rule as a fertility deity. Because the account is extremely fragmentary and conflicting, it is not certain how this was done. In some versions it was the tears of Anat that brought him back from the beyond; in other accounts it was the intervention of Shapesh; in others still it was the "breath of El" himself, which could be interpreted to mean the wind. In some ancient cultures, the wind was often considered to be the breath of the gods, and as such was deemed to have supernatural powers. In other accounts, Ba'al does

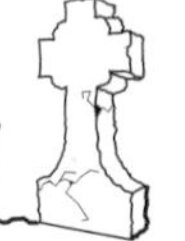

not return from death at all—although these tales probably refer to other incarnations of the god. It is possible that this resurrection myth—that of Ba'al-Hadad—was adopted in part by the Canaanites, and may have influenced early Semitic thinking as well.

Hebrew Legend

For the early Hebrews, the Afterlife was a dark and ill-defined place known as Sheol, from which none could return. The name itself probably comes from the Assyrian *Shu'alu*, meaning "a gathering place" (of the dead), or *shilu*, meaning a chamber (usually underground). It was here that the shades of all the departed—irrespective of whether they had lived an upright life or not—gathered to mill about and eat dirt, which seems to have been the staple diet of the departed, with no real interest in the world that they had left. In this it contained elements of the early Babylonian idea of Kur. Gradually, however, as the Hebrew religion became more sophisticated, new aspects began to creep into the picture, and the idea of an Afterlife began to evolve. Sheol was now comprised of several levels, one of which was a place of punishment and torture for sins that had been committed in the previous existence. This section would later become equated with Gehenna.

Moloch

In reality Gehenna or Gehinnom (*Gai-ben-Hinnom*—the valley of Hinnom's son) actually existed, and was well known to the later Jewish people. It was a steep ravine-line valley that lay outside the walls of Jerusalem, stretching between Mount Zion and the Kidron Valley, which acted as a rubbish dump for the city. It was also a place where the bodies of executed criminals and malefactors, who could not be buried within the city limits, were thrown to be eaten by scavenging animals. It was reported that fires burned there day and night, which were either started by the city officials to dispose of refuse, or from spontaneous combustion brought on by the hot weather and the compacted rubbish itself. The ravine also had a darker connotation, for it was supposed to be the site of Moloch's barbaric worship. Moloch may have been another incarnation of the god Ba'al, because in some texts the deity is rendered as Ba'al-Moloch, a ferocious deity that demanded child sacrifice. This dreadful deity ruled over the valley from an enclosure, which was said to be at its upper end. Small wonder, then, that Gehenna became equated with a place of fire, punishment, and torment into which the wicked and unworthy were cast.

This place served as a forerunner for the Christian notion of Hell; indeed, the later Jews translated the idea of the lower levels of Sheol as Hades in Greek texts. From there there was no return; those who languished there had been cast into the fire to be punished, but there *might* be some sort of return from the upper levels of Sheol or from "the bosom of Abraham," to which the exceptionally righteous went after death. Such a return from the Afterlife may well have been a *physical* one in which the actual cadaver came back in tangible form—although this aspect is left deliberately vague. The notion of returning from the dead—or more specifically, the power to return others from the dead—was gradually transferring itself from gods and supernatural figures to the earth-bound heroes of Semitic religion.

King Saul

Although many of the early Hebrew tales concern themselves with the power of the patriarchs there was one rather ambiguous story of a religious figure being summoned back to the mortal world by magic: King Saul's visit to the famous Witch of Endor. The town of Endor, which allegedly lay on the

The Witch of Endor

northern side of the Jezreel Valley in Lower Galilee, had originally been a Canaanite settlement where, according to tradition, Ba'al had been worshipped, but was now under the control of the Semite tribe of Menesseh. Possibly because of its former Canaanite connections, it had a reputation for the occult and for soothsaying. With his kingdom under threat from the advancing Philistines, who had entered the Jezreel Valley and were ready to face the invaders at the Battle of Mount Gilboa (possibly 1006 BCE), King Saul called upon God for an assurance that he would be victorious. However, God's main spokesperson in Israel, the prophet Samuel, was dead and, because of the monarch's past sins, God refused to answer by other means. According to the Old Testament (1st Samuel 28:1–25), one of the king's servants mentioned a woman who "had a familiar spirit" (translated in Latin as a *Pythoness*—a sorceress or a trafficker with occult arts) who might be able to summon Samuel back from the dead for them. Although Saul himself had outlawed witchcraft in Israel, he agreed, and they visited the alleged witch. In some interpretations the woman possessed a talisman that she used to conjure up the "likeness" of the prophet; in others she may have acted as no more than a conduit through which Samuel returned. But return from the dead he did.

The exact nature of the dead prophet's return from the tomb is unclear. Did he return as a vision or a ghost, or did he return in actual bodily form? Was he summoned by the magic of the witch, or did God allow him to return in order to rebuke the king? Whatever form his return took, he was able to communicate with Saul (some have argued that this was direct communication, others that it was through the witch), and he was able to issue a dire and angry prophesy: Saul would be defeated by the Philistines and the king himself would die. This warning proved to be correct, and is counted as God's retribution on the wayward king. Although there is no indication as to what

befell the revenant prophets after he had uttered his prophesy (presumably he returned to the grave) the incident remains a Biblical example of an individual being called forth from the tomb by supernatural forces.

The actual form that the revenant took is not properly described. The Standard King James Bible translation simply states that it was "an old man covered in a mantle," which the witch sees, but the translation then goes on to state that Saul *saw* that it was Samuel (whom he unquestionably recognized) and that it terrified him. This seems to imply that the returning revenant took on some form of bodily shape, which was recognizably that of the prophet. Whether this form was corporeal or spiritual is a matter for conjecture. Some biblical scholars have argued that this was not in fact Samuel, but some sort of demon that had been drawn to the situation by Saul's previous wickedness, and was seeking to undermine the children of Israel. Again, one cannot be altogether sure.

Gradually, as the Hebrew people became more settled, and, as the Judaic consciousness began to expand and develop some similar stories, testimonials concerning the power of the Hebrew patriarchs began to emerge, and a number of these are found in the Old Testament.

When it came to returning from the dead, some of the departed prophets appeared to have a problem: Some of them had never actually *died* in the traditional sense. In these instances, the phrase that has been used to describe the departure of such figures from this life is *bodily translation*, in which they passed from one sphere of existence into another without actually dying. The implication contained in this translation was that they might return from the Afterlife (being with God) at any time.

Elijah

Although it is quite possible that a number of early heroes were translated in such a fashion, only a couple of stories are now recorded in Semitic and Christian scripture; one of these was the important Hebrew prophet Elijah.

After Abraham, the ninth-century BCE figure of Elijah ranks high amongst all the prophets and patriarchs of both Jewish and Christian traditions. (Elijah was one of the prophets who is reputed to have appeared to Jesus on the Mount of Transfiguration.) He is referred to as a "Tishbite," although there is no geographical location for his homeland. It is thought that the village or settlement of Tishbe, from which he reputedly came, *might* have lain in Gilead—a mountainous region to the east of the River Jordan. However, the term *Tishbite* was also a general one simply meaning "foreigner." He preached at a time of great turmoil and division in the kingdom of Israel, when the cult of Yahweh (Jehovah) was becoming more firmly established in the Semitic consciousness.

He is perhaps most famous for his denunciation of Jezebel, the Phoenician wife of King Ahab of Israel, who had brought foreign worship into the country, and for his confrontation with her priests (the priests of Ba'al-Malkart of Tyre—the city from which she came). In this, he is seen as the conscience of an emerging faith, and therefore takes his place as one of its chief exponents. It was natural, therefore, that he should have some supernatural elements and powers associated with him. One of these miraculous attributes was the power to raise the dead. This power was demonstrated later. After speaking out against Jezebel, Elijah fled to avoid the wrath of Ahab and hid briefly by the brook Cherith (identified by some as the Wadi-el-Kelt near Jerusalem) before leaving Israel for the Phoenician town of Zerephath (Serepath), which lay

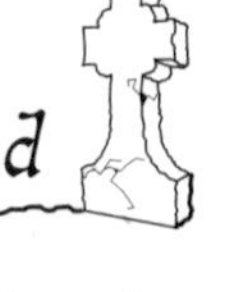

between the cities of Tyre and Sidon on the Mediterranean coast. There he lodged with a Phoenician widow and her young son who were extremely good to him. However, the widow's son became sick and died. The widow begged Elijah to restore him to life, which the prophet eventually did by using a supernatural power that God had allegedly given him. It is assumed that he restored the child to full health, as the Bible (I Kings 17:22) tells us no different. What became of him is unknown, but it is presumed that he continued to live quite normally in Zerephath for many years afterward.

Besides having the power to raise from the dead, Elijah himself was not destined to die in the traditional manner; his departure from this world was rather spectacular. He was walking one day on the banks of the River Jordan together with his friend Elisha, who would succeed him. Desiring to cross the river, Elijah held out his staff; the waters parted so that the two of them could cross on dry land. As they crossed, a great chariot drawn by horses of fire descended from the heavens, and Elijah was carried up in a whirlwind. His cloak fell to the ground, but was picked up by Elisha, who put it on and therefore became the next prophet of Israel. The translation of Elijah meant that the prophet could return from "the Bosom of Abraham" at any time, and indeed in the Christian tradition we are told that both John the Baptist and Jesus were at times mistaken for the resurrected prophet.

Enoch

According to both Jewish and Christian traditions, Enoch was another patriarch who had the same fate as Elijah. Enoch was a direct descendant of Adam and a forefather of Noah. A somewhat mystical figure, he is said to have lived between 3284 and 3017 BCE, departing this life when he was almost

Metatron

300 years old. He appears to have been a man of great faith, and, because of this, God promised him that he should not taste death and so at the end of his long life he was translated. The book of Genesis tells us that "Enoch walked with the Lord and was not," probably meaning that he was carried directly into Heaven. The *Talmud* would also suggest that Enoch was transformed into an

angel named Metatron, and he became part of the Host gathered around the Throne of God. Allegedly, he was the only angel allowed to sit within the Heavenly Precincts (a privilege reserved for God alone) and he appears to have had great power. According to Rabbinical tradition, his flesh became flame; his veins became fire; his lashes became flashes of lightning; and his eyes became flaming torches—a quite startling transformation indeed! Much mystical and magical lore has been attached to Enoch's name, and several books of sorcery, which are of supernatural origin, are ascribed to him. A number of these books reputedly carry incantations designed specifically for summoning the angel Metatron (the translated body of Enoch himself) from beyond the grave and bending the heavenly entity to one's will.

The power to raise people from the dead, as exemplified in the prophet Elijah, was passed on to his successor Elisha. Elisha raised the child of a Shunamite woman who had shown both Elisha and his servant Gaichazi great kindness. According to the tale Elisha lodged at the house of the woman and her husband in Kfar Shunam while he carried out his ministry in the region. As he lodged there, the prophet sensed a great longing in the woman, for the couple had no children and her husband was very old. When he left, the woman refused any form of payment for her kindness, but the prophet promised that they would have a son shortly afterward. Two years later, however, the small boy fell victim to heatstroke and died. Distraught, the woman sent for Elisha, who was some distance away, and begged the holy man to restore the child to life. Elisha was unable to go at that particular time, but sent his servant Gaichazi to visit the woman and perform the miracle. The servant was unsuccessful, so Elisha himself went and bent over the boy's bed, putting his mouth to that of the child and whispering the name of Hashem, a mystical name for God. The boy sneezed, woke up, and came back to life. Why the prophet used such an

The Ephraimites

obscure name for God and not the conventional Yahweh is worthy of note—it may be that the Shunamite was not a Hebrew, or it may be that it was part of a magical spell or incantation to summon the boy back from death.

With some modifications, this story bears a striking resemblance to the tale of Elijah and the widow's son, and it is possible that the two stories might have come from the same source. It might also be possible to argue that they both come from a much earlier source concerning Mesopotamian "wonder-workers," which had been attributed to the two Semitic patriarchs.

Ezekiel

Yet another of the early Prophets who is supposed to have seen the dead rise was Ezekiel. He has been always been something of a mystery, because so little is known about him, and many biblical scholars now agree that, because of the variation in both style and tone, the book of Ezekiel in the Old Testament (which only mentions his name twice) was probably written by more than one man and was compiled about 597 BCE. Nothing is known of his birth or background, though he describes himself as a priest or as the son of a priest—some sources say that he was the son of the Prophet Jeremiah. The book was brought together—perhaps by a person represented by Ezekiel—among a group of Semitic exiles in a place known as Tel-abib on the banks of the Chebar River "in the land of the Chaldeans." These people were fugitives from Babylonian captivity when Babylonian forces had overthrown King Jeconiah of Israel and carried off many of his people into slavery in Babylon.

In the book of Ezekiel, God took the Prophet into a valley through which human bones were scattered. The book of Ezekiel gives no location for this place, nor does it explain to whom the dead bones might have belonged. However, it has been suggested that they belonged to the Ephraimites, which was one of the tribes of Israel that fled from captivity in Egypt before the arrival of Moses and Aaron. God then asked Ezekiel a question: "Son of Man. Can these bones live?" Ezekiel replied that only God Himself knew. Upon this statement, God commanded the Prophet to prophesy over the bones, so that they might live. As Ezekiel prophesied, sinews and flesh were added to the dry bones so that they were bodies, but had no life. God told Ezekiel to prophesy again, and a great wind—the breath of God that had supernatural properties—blew through the valley. The bodies rose once again to join the living. This was counted as one of the greatest miracles of Ezekiel's career, and the one for which he is best remembered.

Many biblical students now take the previous story as allegorical—symbolising the rebirth of the people of Israel after a period of Babylonian captivity. For many fundamentalist Christians, however, the story is factual, and they believe that, through His supernatural power, God did actually raise a valley of dead bones—restoring them to life. The raising of the dead in the valley, they argue, represents the eternal power of God and His superiority over life and death. Whatever the reality of the situation, the idea of supernatural resurrection (mainly at the behest of Yahweh or God) was therefore becoming imbedded in both Jewish and Christian traditions.

Christianity

The notion of raising the dead was not solely confined to the early Hebrew leaders and prophets. Jesus Christ also allegedly performed such miracles during the course of his ministry on earth, and, of course, reputedly returned from the grave after being crucified. This indeed has laid the foundations of a religion that has lasted more than 2,000 years.

One of those who was brought back from the dead by Christ was the daughter of Jairus, described as a high-ranking official in the synagogue. The story is recorded in three of the Synoptic Gospels—Mark, Luke, and Matthew—and follows roughly the same story.

While Jesus was preaching, Jairus approached him and, falling down before him, asked him to come and "lay hands" on his daughter who was ill and close to dying. Because Jesus was considered to be a great healer, he hoped that this would restore her to health. While Jesus was on his way to Jairus's house, a servant arrived telling him that the girl had died. Taking either a couple of his disciples or the girl's grieving parents with him, Jesus went into the room where the child lay. Bending over the bed, Jesus took her by the hand and reputedly said in Aramaic, "*Talitha Qumi,*" which means "Little girl, arise." The child awoke and got up, fully restored to life. However, this miracle is disputed by some biblical scholars who claim that it wasn't a resurrection from the dead at all. They point out that, although Mark and Luke seem to be in agreement (Mark 5:21–24; 35–42 and Luke 40–42; 49–56), the Gospel of Matthew (Matthew 9:18–26) takes a slightly different stance, omitting the crucial statement that the girl was dead. The suggestion is that she was merely ill and had recovered by the time that Jesus had arrived. This, it has been argued, casts doubt about the particular "miracle" and the alleged "resurrection."

Lazarus

There is also a dispute about another of Jesus's resurrection miracles—that of Lazarus (or Elaezar) of Bethany, although it is unclear as to exactly who Lazarus actually was. In the biblical account he lived in the small town of Bethany, and was the brother of Mary Magdalene (one of the Jesus' more prominent female followers) and their sister Martha. However, some traditions (largely medieval but citing earlier sources) assert that he was the brother of the Virgin Mary and therefore Jesus' earthly uncle. Other legends describe him as a Cypriot living with his sisters, who all became followers and friends of Jesus. The relationship between Jesus and Lazarus seems to have been very deep, because when he heard of Lazarus's death, Jesus wept openly. When he arrived in Bethany he found that Lazarus had already been laid in the tomb. Jesus then told his sister Martha that he was sure that Lazarus would rise again. Jesus ordered the stone to be rolled away from the entrance to the tomb and cried with a loud voice, "Lazarus! Come forth!" whereupon the cadaver appeared at the mouth of the tomb, still clad in his burial clothes. Jesus ordered the shroud-wrappings to be removed, and it was discovered that Lazarus was alive and had indeed risen from the dead at Jesus' command. This was widely accepted as a symbol of His divinity, and was cited as one of his greatest miracles. The story appeared in the Gospel of John (11:1–45). What became of Lazarus thereafter is unknown. The Bible remains remarkably silent on his subsequent existence—although there have been a number of legends.

Some stories say that Lazarus was reviled by his neighbors because he had cheated death and was forced to flee to Cyprus (hence, the Cypriot connection of the later tales) where he became bishop of Larnaka/Kittim, and was specifically appointed to the post by the apostles Paul and Barnabas. The bishops of Kittim had a special status: They were autocephaletic, which means that they did not report to any higher authority and acted as functioning rulers. Another story, recounted in the 13th-century *Golden Legend,* states that directly after the Crucifixion, Lazarus and Mary Magdalene fled with some friends from the Holy Land to Europe, where Lazarus became the first bishop of Marseilles. Other parts of France also appear to claim him as well; for example, he is also cited as bishop of Vezelay in Burgundy, while the Abbey of

the Trinity in Vendome at one time was said to hold a phylactery (the Jewish name was *tefilin*) allegedly containing a tear of Christ, which had been shed at the tomb of Lazarus. In neighboring Autun he was extolled as Saint Lazere and the church in the town was dedicated to him. Saint Lazere, according to legend, was also incredibly old, outliving most men in the surrounding area. This was presumably attributed to the fact that he had apparently been raised from the dead. In all of these legends, Lazarus continued to live a normal life after being resurrected by becoming a prominent churchman.

Jesus Christ

Arguably, the greatest resurrection miracle in Western belief was, of course, the rising of Jesus Christ, an alleged event that has laid the foundations for the Christian religion. The core of this belief is that Jesus was crucified, died on the Cross, and was buried in a tomb. However, on the third day after his crucifixion it is believed that he rose again, and this event was witnessed by a section of his followers. Believers say that this event is the ultimate proof of his divinity and union with God. Indeed, it is often proclaimed that Jesus "conquered" death through his own will and sense of purpose. Many fundamentalist believers assert that this was an actual bodily resurrection and that Jesus returned "in the flesh" and not as a spirit or ghost. In other words, he was resurrected in tangible form. Jesus appeared several times to his followers, and in one account (John 20:24–29) a follower named Thomas (also called Didymus) asked him for physical proof of his bodily return from the grave. Jesus therefore invited him to place his fingers in the holes in his hand, made by the nails at the Crucifixion, or to thrust his hand into the wound made by the lance of a Roman soldier who stood beside the Cross. Whether or not Thomas did this is not revealed in the Bible, but the invitation alone seemed to have been enough to convince him of Jesus' bodily form. Strangely, none of the other followers appear to have questioned the nature of Jesus' corporality.

Of course, there has been much theological debate about the exact nature of the resurrection story. Fundamentalist Christians have strongly argued that it was an actual bodily event and, as evidence, point to the fact that in one of his appearances after death, Jesus actually sat down and ate a meal with two witnesses. Today some Christians assert that the resurrection was not an actual physical event, but rather a symbolic embodiment of the aspirations and belief of the Christian people. Although it is not the intention of this book to become embroiled in theological controversy, the resurrection story does give one of the strongest examples in modern belief of an individual's return from the dead. It is a story that had been passed down for more than 2,000 years, and one that had formed one of the central tenets of an established church. For believers, Jesus actually conquered death, and remains the only person who returned from the grave through His own spiritual will and the purity of His existence on earth.

And yet such a belief is slightly ambiguous, because, as we have seen, the raising of the dead and restoration of life seems to be a rather well-established belief in both the Jewish and Christian traditions. Indeed, in Orthodox Jewish law the resurrection of the dead by various rabbis remains the last of the 13 Precepts advocated by the philosopher and theologian Moses Maimonides (1135–1204), who taught in Anatolia, Morocco, and parts of Egypt. He states: "I believe with the complete faith that there will be Techiat Hameitim—the revival of the dead—whenever it will be God's (blessed be He) desire to arise and do so."

Maimonides suggests that by calling on Yahweh's (God's) name any holy rabbi might be able to raise the dead or perhaps even return from the dead

himself in accordance with God's wishes. This idea was later assimilated as a rule of law into some forms of rabbinical teaching and codes of practice. These rabbis were considered to be the successors to the prophets, and it firmly established the notion of resurrection by supernatural means within the Hebrew and Jewish traditions.

The idea of raising the dead was being established within the Christian tradition, too. Not only had Jesus allegedly brought individuals back to life and had come back from the dead himself, but he instructed his followers to heal lepers, cast out spirits, and raise the dead through the power of God in the style of the prophets of old. It was also one of the "gifts" that were, according to the New Testament, given to the apostles when the Holy Spirit descended upon them at pentecost. The fathers of the Church, who were the apostles' successors, reputedly carried on this tradition. Within the teachings of the Catholic Church, a number of saints are credited with miraculously raising the dead—symbolizing their holiness and God's mercy. These include St. Francis Xavier, St. Rose of Lima (the first saint to be born on American soil), and the Blessed Margaret of Castello, who was said to be a midget, a hunchback, blind, and lame. However, despite all of these things, she supposedly raised a number of deceased victims of a deadly plague that was sweeping Italy in the 13th century. Throughout the Middle Ages, many localized saints and religious people were also credited with such powers, and although many of them are now discounted, they formed a distinct corpus of lore within the Christian tradition that persisted throughout the West across the centuries.

Celtic Mythology

So far we have looked at the notion of returning from the dead in early Middle Eastern and Semitic mythology, and this is certainly the area in which many of these original myths arose. There is also, however, a similar tradition among the Celtic peoples, which has made the Semitic ideal of resurrection more easily assimilated in some areas, such as the central tenet of the Christian faith as it began to move across the Celtic lands. Indeed, the notions of death and resurrection (rebirth or renewal) were central to the Celtic perception of the world. The Celts, who settled in Western Europe, were largely an agricultural people who viewed existence in the form of a great wheel that turned through the world of the living and the dead throughout the course of the year—giving rise, of course, to the seasons. Thus, in summer, everything was green, vibrant, and bursting with life, but soon it began to wither and die as autumn and winter set in. In the heart of winter, the ground was hard, frosty, and seeming sterile—nothing would grow and the very world itself seemed dead. But the wheel turned, and subsequently life returned in the spring; buds burst forth and foliage blossomed. This, to the Celtic mind, was a return to life after the death of winter—it was the natural way of things. And if this ideal could be applied to the world all around, then surely it could also be applied to individuals as well.

This ideal tied in with another persistent notion among the Celts—that, as farmers, they were somehow the actual physical embodiment of the landscape within which they lived. This was especially relevant in the case of a local ruler or monarch who was believed to be the landscape in physical form, or, at the very least, inextricably connected to the area over which they ruled. Consequently, no monarch could rule if he or she had a blemish on his or her body, because his or her body was supposed to reflect the land. An ancient Irish king, known as Conn of the Hundred Battles, had to step down from the throne when he lost an eye in a conflict, just in case his facial disfigurement would blight his realm in some way. Not only were the Celtic monarchs a part of the

land, but they were also closely connected to the seasons. As the monarch grew older, he or she became more stooped, grayer, and feebler, moving toward death. There was a fear among the subjects that the monarch's frailty might be reflected in the land—there might be droughts, the winters might be more severe, and so on. The monarch had to die and then return to life, thus ensuring that warmth and greenery would return to land, and the crops would be plentiful. This translated into what may have been a ritual killing of the aging monarch, with another younger person to inherit the spirit that the old ruler had embodied. Thus, the legends of the King of the Wood, Green Jack, and The Green Man were born. The returning king symbolized good fortune for his people and ensured that the landscape remained verdant and vibrant. Resurrection and the return to life also symbolized prosperity for the people, and paralleled the Wheel of the Year.

And it may not only have been monarchs who returned from the grave (albeit perhaps symbolically). The Celtic peoples also believed that mighty warriors might be revived from the dead after being slain on the battlefield provided they were anointed with some form of magic. Initially such magic was contained in elements such as water.

Water

In ancient Celtic lore—as in the traditions of other cultures—water was a special element with great cleansing and restorative powers, but it also had power of life and death. In the prehistoric legend of the Sons of Partholon, the four protagonists had ridden out on a quest to find the fabled Waters of Oblivion, which could both kill and restore in equal measure. On finding the fountain, three of them approached it without reciting the appropriate incantations, and were all slain as soon as they drank it. Hearing of the tragedy and assuming that all his sons were dead (therefore there was no successor), Partholon himself committed suicide, overcome with grief. However, his youngest son (who had survived) gave him the Waters to drink and restored him to life, after which he continued to reign for many years—perhaps a metaphor for the death and resurrection of the king in many traditions—including Celtic. The legend, which is extremely old, may have formed the base of some Semitic, Roman, and Greek tales, and may even have been Mesopotamian in origin. The name may also have been a variation of Partholon, an ancient Greek king who is supposed to have fled Greece and come to Ireland in some former time. The idea of the Waters of Oblivion, however, may have laid the foundation for the belief that the element could take away disease and maybe even restore life itself.

In Scottish legend, too, the Dalriadic king Fergus McErc (Dalriada was an ancient Celtic kingdom that stretched between the north of Ireland and the west coast of Scotland), was dying of leprosy and was told by a Highland witch that, if he washed his face is a certain well in Ireland, he would be cured and his life would be saved. Fergus knew where the well might be, so he set out for it. However, during a storm, the ship was drive off course and was wrecked on the Irish coast, drowning all the crew, including the king himself. The place where he met his end, however, is still known as Fergus's Rock (Carrig Fergus)—in the Antrim town of Carrickfergus. But the legend of the well with its wonderful powers still remained.

The notions of water being associated with immortality appear in many cultures. We have only to think of the Fountain of Youth, sought after by the Spanish explorer and founder of the state of Florida, Juan Ponce de Leon, back in the 1500s, to grasp the significance of this mystical and miraculous element.

The Cauldron of Goibniu

Celtic Lore

In Celtic lore, such a belief appears. In his *General Topography of Ireland,* the monk Geraldus Cambrensis, who came to Ireland in 1185 as Confessor to Prince John, recounts a story about a certain lake in Munster, which could restore youth. If a man washed his hair in its waters, Gerald declared, though it is gray, it would be restored to its natural color. Of course, we need to treat most of what Gerald says with extreme skepticism; he was extremely gullible and believed even the wildest, imaginative stories about Ireland—but his story does serve to show that the idea of water and the ideas of restoration, renewal, and immortality were closely linked in the Celtic mind.

From the idea of immortality, cleansing, and the banishing of illness and disease, it was only a small step to linking water sources with the return and revival from the dead. If certain wells could take away potentially fatal diseases, such as the leprosy, that affected Fergus McErc, then perhaps others might even restore a dead person to life again. Similar to the Fountain of Youth, some wells therefore became associated with immortality; these were scattered throughout the Celtic world and the locations of most of them have been lost. There was said, for example, to be a well in Brittany, France, which was guarded by Druids, where men could regain their youth and be restored to life if need be. It was said that elderly men were placed in its waters, and after having done so, emerged as young babies. The well was said to be Pagan—sacred to ancient Celtic gods—and so it was destroyed by the monks from the monastery at Cluny, who saw it as an affront to Christianity and a mockery of Jesus sacrifice for Mankind. Another such well was said to exist somewhere in Wales, and was apparently visited by a number of ancient kings—including King Arthur.

Cauldrons

As time passed, the idea of a well began to change and became slightly more sophisticated. It was replaced, in the popular mind, by the image of a cauldron or a pot. The word *cauldron* has its origins in the Irish word (derived from early Celtic) *coire, coiri,* or *ceare* (there are many variants in spelling), which simply meant "a vessel for holding liquid"; some whirlpools and deep-sea caverns are sometimes referred to as "cauldrons." This is also the root of our word *chalice*, and it has always been associated with centrality, ritual, and the abundance of life. Indeed, the notion of a life-giving cauldron—often referred to as "The Cauldron of Rebirth"—a great utensil within which warriors slain in battle might be supernaturally restored to life—is featured in a number of Celtic legends and tales.

Cauldrons or great cooking pots were often central facets of Celtic life, and it is known that there were a number of ceremonial vessels that may have been used for feasting during special occasions. They were associated with full stomachs and well being, life, and vitality. Many were said to resemble a womb or container in which life might start. It is not surprising, therefore, that they were also associated with rebirth, resurrection, and renewal. According to Gerald of Wales, a mystical cauldron was used in the inauguration of kings of Ulster in a ceremony that also symbolized death and rebirth. After ritual intercourse with a white mare, which was then slaughtered, the prospective monarch was placed in a cauldron where he was fed the mare's meat in order to "fatten" him up. He was then symbolically "cooked," emerging as a new and reinvigorated being who was ready to rule his people. Whether Gerald actually witnessed this ceremony is open to question, but the story serves to demonstrate that the tradition connecting the cauldron to the notion of resurrection was very much alive in the Celtic mind.

In a tale from the second branch of the Welsh *Mabinogion*, for example, Branwen, the sister of Bran, the ancient giant and king (described as "Bran the Blessed—King of England") was given in marriage to Matholwch, an Irish king. As the festivities were in full swing, Bran's irascible half-brother Efnisen arrived unexpectedly and asked what the occasion might be. On hearing that his half-sister had been given in marriage without asking his consent, Efnisen flew into a terrible rage and mutilated all of Matholwch's horses. In recompense Bran offered him a number of items, including a great and magical cauldron, which, if a dead warrior was put into it, he would live again, completely whole as before, although he would not have the power of speech. This Bran had obtained from a giantess whom he had rescued from a fire in an iron house, and to whom the king had shown a kindness. The gift may have been a variant of the Sacred Cauldron of Goibniu, which was forged by a giant out of magic metal in the earliest times; the cauldron could produce food, heal, and even restore the dead to life. Matholwch seemed satisfied with the compensation and returned to Ireland with his bride. Some of his men, however, still grumbled over the mutilation of the horses, and said that Bran and Efnisen had got off far too lightly. Some of the Irish nobles resolved to make war on Bran at the first opportunity.

Back in Ireland, Matholwch treated Branwen abominably, forcing Bran to lead a troop of warriors from Wales to support his sister. In another variant of the tale, Matholwch contemplated putting Branwen's son Gwern on the Irish throne and a number of nobles rose up and threatened him, forcing Bran's army to threaten Ireland. A peace was hammered out between the two kings but the Irish nobles saw their chance. They decided to hide in meal sacks that Bran was taking back with him, and surprise the British king and possibly kill him. Efnisen, however, got wind of their plans and had the British warriors run

the sacks through with their swords, killing all within. Such slaughter could not be allowed to pass without retaliation, and a war broke out between Britain and Ireland. The cauldron that had been given in compensation to Matholwch now became very important, for the Irish simply gathered up their fallen, placed them in the pot, and they sprang out alive again. In this way, the Irish forces never diminished, although those of the Britons and Welsh—who had no such cauldron—did.

However, the cunning Efnisen came up with a plan. He lay down among the dead, was gathered up, and placed in the cauldron. Once inside he began to expand himself, pushing on the sides of the cauldron until it burst asunder. With the cauldron broken, the Irish could not revive their dead and the sides were evened up once more. The battle that followed was long and bloody, and in the end Bran triumphed, but was severely wounded and had only seven men left. He returned to England, where he died, his body buried in present-day London. The fragments of the cauldron were gathered together and buried, so that no man might use them again.

Although this is perhaps one of the best-known tales concerning such a cauldron and its power to raise men from the dead, there is no doubt that there were other stories about such artifacts from earlier times. As has already been noted, the cauldron was usually the center of the household or the feast, and was the symbol of fecundity and plenty. It would later be translated into the image of a horn, becoming the Horn of Plenty, which is featured in many legends from ancient times.

Just as the sons of Partholon rode out searching for the Waters of Oblivion, so there are hints of other quests in the prehistoric world, with the protagonists trying to find such wonderful cauldrons and containers in order to bring prosperity and immortality to their communities. It was generally assumed—as with the magic cauldron of Bran—that such vessels had been forged by the giants in some dim and distant time but had since been lost and now lay somewhere in the world. The Cauldron of Rebirth therefore became an almost unobtainable "quest item" among many ancient peoples and cultures. However, the perception of the cauldron was about to undergo another change throughout Europe as the times changed once again.

The quest for the Cauldron of Rebirth was in many respects a Pagan one—the item was closely associated with heathen ritual, and therefore it did not sit easily with the emerging Christian faith that was beginning to establish itself across Western Europe. The quest for the Cauldron began to morph into something else as the new faith took hold and the magical pot became a religious vessel that would intrigue Christendom to the present day. The Cauldron of Rebirth became the Holy Grail, and the quest for the Pagan artifact would become transformed into the romantic search for the sacred icon throughout medieval times and beyond.

Search for the Holy Grail

The Grail has long occupied a central place in Christian mythology. The name comes from the ancient French word *graal*, meaning "a deep serving dish or platter." In other words, it may have started out as a large container, capable of serving many men, such as the cauldron. In medieval Christian romance, however, it became a cup, though explanations of its origins and functions are often somewhat contradictory. For some it was the wine cup, blessed by Jesus at the Last Supper, but for others it was the sacred receptacle that had caught some of his blood at the foot of the Cross, held by either the

Virgin Mary or Joseph of Arimathea (a wealthy follower who had donated a tomb in which to lay Jesus' body). In either respect it was considered an extremely holy object throughout the Christian world and in many respects a symbol of Jesus himself. The Grail was now believed to be lost, and so formed the basis of many quests to find it.

The idea of the dead and resurrected Jesus symbolized in a cup fit in well with older myths and beliefs, particularly with the idea of the Cauldron of Life. The notion of blood being shed for his people—a central tenet of the Christian faith—paralleled the idea of the Pagan king dying and then rising again to bring well being and salvation to his people. Life could once again emerge out of the death of the Divine Protagonist; even the language surrounding Christianity contained these elements. Today certain Protestant sectors of the Christian church speak about being "born again," "resurrected in Christ," or "restored to life everlasting," which perhaps dates back to the early Pagan concepts embodied in the early stories of the Grail. To drink from the sacred cup reputedly restored youth, granted immortality, and returned to life those that were dead. In effect, it was the Christian embodiment of many old Pagan beliefs.

In accordance with its prominence in Christian iconography, the lost Grail was generally supposed to be located somewhere in Western Europe where Christianity had taken hold. Some traditions, of course, held that it was still somewhere in the Holy Land, but the general consensus was that it had been brought to Europe by returning Crusaders or perhaps by someone much earlier.

Indeed, some legends state that the Grail was brought to England (then the far-flung corner of the Roman Empire) by Joseph of Arimathea, who had fled from the Middle East to avoid Roman persecution in the days after Jesus' crucifixion. Other legends state that it was brought to England by Jesus himself following the Resurrection. Some English traditions state that it was taken to Glastonbury in Somerset and placed somewhere near the Tor, which, at the time, was an island called Ynys-witrin, or Glass Island. In Arthurian tradition this was given as one of the sites for the mythical land of Avalon. This, however, was probably no more than a legend made up by the monks of Glastonbury Abbey in later years to raise funds for their foundation; they also claimed that King Arthur was buried there. Joseph of Arimathea was said to be the founder of Glastonbury Abbey, and a tree that blossomed close by was said to have grown from his staff that he had planted in the ground. In a variant of the Grail legend it was in fact King Arthur who had brought the sacred cup to Glastonbury, and few monarchs are as closely connected with the quest for the Grail as he.

If the Grail did indeed come to England, then its first guardian was not Arthur, but a giant Celtic warrior named Bron. In most variants of the tale, Bron was primarily a Christian warrior, but it is, of course, evident that he was based upon the legend of Bran in the tale from the *Mabinogion*, who was given the magic cauldron by the giant hag. In some versions of the tale, Bron was also considered to be the guardian of life and death who could, through the power of the Grail, restore the dead to life. In fact, he may have been a Christian representation of a much more ancient Pagan god.

A later custodian, dating from medieval times, was the Fisher King who dwelt in a castle in the middle of a wasteland. He was partially crippled because of a wound on his side that never healed, and he supposedly served as the custodian of a number of religious objects—one being a spear, the point of which ran with blood (the spear of the Roman centurion Longinus, which had pierced the side of Jesus as he hung on the Cross perhaps), and another being the Grail. This was often borne by a maiden and was a supernatural

source of nourishment for all those around, as well as being restorative and able to resurrect from the dead. In some versions the Fisher King's father dwelt in another room from his son, subsisting on a single Mass wafer, which was placed daily at its door. There are some who equate the person of the Fisher King with Joseph of Arimathea himself, declaring that he drank from the Grail and therefore could not die. No one knew where the Fisher King's castle lay except that it might lie somewhere within the British Isles.

The quest for this castle and for the Grail became a central theme of later Arthurian romance. According to legend, Sir Perceval accidentally stumbled upon the Fisher King's caste, which supposedly lay within a remote part of King Arthur's realm. He brought back the tale of the mysterious fortress and its bizarre inhabitant to the monarch's court at Camelot. Seated at a meeting at the famous Round Table, Arthur and his knights then received a vision of the Grail that formed the basis of their quest for the sacred vessel. In Christian tradition, the gathering was of course evocative of Jesus and his disciples, gathered around the table at the Last Supper or even of the disciples themselves gathered together in a house when the Holy Spirit descended upon them. Such Christian symbolism was not lost in Arthurian legend. In other versions of the story Arthur was old and close to death, and it was considered that perhaps the Grail might rejuvenate him and restore him to life. He would then reward the knight who found it. Only one knight at the Table, however, would do so. This turned out to be Galahad, son of Lancelot, who was the only one of the company without sin, so was pure enough to see and hold the cup.

Much of the cohesive Arthurian romance derives from the works of Thomas Malory (c1405–1471), whose *Morte d'Arthur* collected a number of both French and English traditions; however, the story had been around long before that.

Indeed in the earliest known tale by Chrétien de Troyes, a French troubadour and poet of the early 12th century, what Percival saw at the castle of the Fisher King was not a holy goblet but simply a deep and womb-like dish or pot similar to a cauldron, remindful of the Cauldron of Rebirth, which could raise the dead. According to Chrétien, the graal that Percival saw was a supernatural object with special powers, but those powers are not disclosed in the work. In many of the early writings (such as those of Robert de Boron that appeared around 1200) the graal is not thought of as a particularly holy relic in the same way that some fragments of the True Cross were perceived. Nevertheless, it was said to have supernatural powers (though whether or not these were explicitly connected with Christianity is unclear), which may have been linked to older fertility magic and may have included the power to restore life to the dead. Perhaps it is for this reason that the Church never formally accepted the idea of the Grail as a Christian relic, and instead consigned it simply to the areas of popular medieval romance.

The chivalric search to find the Grail—popular at many medieval courts—was probably based on older quest tales concerning the Cauldron of Rebirth. The most famous of these was Arthur's quest to find the "Spoils of Arawn," which is recounted in the First Branch of the *Mabinogion.* In this tale, Pwyll, Lord of Dyfed in Wales, traded places with Arawn, Lord of the Underworld, and received from him a magical cauldron that would not boil the food of a coward, but would miraculously restore the dead to life. In this version, women of exceptional wisdom and power guard the Cauldron, and only a fraction of Arthur's knights return from the quest. This story was probably the template for the romance of the Grail, thus linking the holy artifact of later Christian legend with the Pagan tradition.

Whether it was the Holy Grail or the Cauldron of Rebirth that restored the dead to life, the idea of bodily resurrection from the tomb had been established in the human psyche. The tradition had begun in the early Semitic and Arab worlds with the corporeal restoration of ancient gods after a period in the Underworld. These beliefs later became firmly rooted in the Christian tradition through the physical Resurrection of Jesus, which, in many respects, seems to have been a furtherance of that earlier belief. Gods and great heroes, it seemed, might return from the grave at any time. The notion of such returns was linked with the idea of immortality and of continuing at least some form of existence even after death had claimed the individual. Of course, there were similar notions in some other cultures as well, and we shall look at these shortly. However, the established tradition of physical return from the grave would grow and develop as the centuries progressed, particularly in Western Europe, incorporating a number of other ideas into that belief; it is to that cultural continuation that we now turn.

2

When Churchyards Yawn

It was not only the gods and heroes of the ancient world for whom death was not really the end. As time passed and civilizations became more sophisticated, there was also an emerging tradition that certain ordinary people might also escape the clutches of the grave, return in a corporeal state. Indeed, in some cultures, death was viewed as something akin to sleep, where the body lay in a suspended state, but might arise at any time to resume a kind of sporadic quasi-life in general society. In parts of the Nordic world where such beliefs were held, small houses were often built where the body of the deceased "lived" in a suspended condition. These "dead houses" were often made of stone and were usually constructed by a community to contain the bodies of great warriors or powerful local chieftains. From time to time, these great and mighty men would rise from their houses either to return to their earthly homes or to wander about the countryside, either alone or in the company of others who were similarly dead. Many of these wanderings occurred at night, and encounters with them often seem to have been incredibly dangerous and violent. Although sometimes counted as ghosts, they were not the insubstantial wraiths of later centuries of which most of us are familiar, but rather they were corporeal in nature and could usually inflict very real harm to those against whom they took a spite or a dislike.

Draugr and Other Legends

Such wandering dead were known to the Vikings as *draugr*. The name itself may have been Icelandic in origin and may have initially referred to powerful magicians who seemed to be able to return after death to their homes for limited periods. (Iceland was famous for its magical traditions and allegedly boasted a number of secretive "black schools" where the magical arts were taught by necromancers and others.) The idea, however, quickly spread across the Scandinavian world and became associated not only with magicians, but also with warriors and berserkers. The majority of the tales that have come down to us were initially written by Icelandic monks, but have been adapted to fit locations in other Scandinavian countries and other parts of the Viking world, such as France and Britain. Draugr were often instantly recognizable by the color of their skin, which was either black as death (a sign of purification perhaps) or corpse-white. Many of them appear to have gone around in groups creating panic and mayhem wherever they went—just as they might have done when alive—and should not be approached for any reason. As soon as it was daylight, however, they returned to their "dead houses" in order to rest before the next night's activities.

Stories of this form of walking dead have come down to us in a series of great sagas (which were actually collections of tales that had been told by local *skelds*—historians, folklorists, or bards), which circulated in Scandinavia around the 11th and 12th centuries. The most famous of these is the *Eyrbyggja Saga*, which was probably written at the Icelandic monastery of Helgafell around the early 11th century.

One of the central tales concerns a dead warrior by the name of Thorolf Halt-Foot who had been greatly feared during his lifetime. Even in death, he would not "lie still" and took to rampaging around the countryside. Indeed it had been widely expected that, because of his wild lifestyle, death would not restrain him, and it was taken as an evil omen when, during the summer months directly after his death, cattle grazing near his dead house began to sicken, then went mad and died. It was further noted that birds that landed on the roof of the tomb also fell down dead. Shortly after Thorolf had been interred, a herdsman was found dead a little ways from the tomb site, and it was assumed that the draugr had now risen from his grave and was wandering about. The dead man's body was completely blue and every bone in his body had been broken by an incredibly violent assault. There was no doubt in local minds that this was an attack of a draugr and that the animated corpse was that of Thorolf.

All through the winter, the walking cadaver terrorized the surrounding countryside, appearing outside several houses in the district. He was allegedly seen close to the house of the herdsman that he allegedly killed, driving the dead man's wife mad with fear. She subsequently collapsed and died with the stress of it all and ironically was buried close to the dead house where

Thorolf himself lay. After this, the draugr became even more lively and violent, actually breaking into the surrounding houses and assaulting the inhabitants as they lay sleeping. At some stage he seems to have been joined by several more undead companions, forming a kind of "gang" that roamed around the countryside, causing distress and mayhem. This could not be tolerated and, in the end, the community, led by members of the Church, made stern representations to his son, Arnkel, to have something done about the riotous revenant of his father. Together with a posse of friends Arnkel went to the barrow where Thorolf lay, broke it open, and removed the body, placing it in a yoke between two oxen. They had intended to take the corpse to a lonely place and destroy it, but Thorolf's corpse was heavy, and they were all exhausted. They took him instead to a distant headland, and there they laid him into the earth with Arnkel himself building a little wall to keep the cadaver restrained in case he should rise again. The place was almost inaccessible, and it was thereafter shunned by decent folk.

Although the tale of Thorolf Halt-Foot is one of the most complete stories that has been passed down to us, it is by no means the only one. The *Laxdoela Saga,* for instance, includes the story of a warrior named Hrapp who returned from the grave as a violent and animated corpse. In *Gettir's Saga,* Gettir had to fight with a draugr that emerged from the tomb of a chieftain named Kar the Old. Gettir finally defeated the corpse, but exhuming the body, striking the head off with a single blow of his axe, and burning the body together with Kar's artifacts in a great bonfire was far from the end. It is worth noting that great carte had to be taken not to inhale the smoke from any of these fires, for those who did might become draugr themselves when they died. This method for destroying the walking dead and preventing them from rising again was exactly the same as those traditionally used for destroying vampires in parts of Eastern Europe in the Middle Ages.

Vikings

Viking stories of the walking dead often had a profound influence on the areas that they visited and settled. Consequently, tales of the walking dead—fostering a belief in the subject—also appear in the texts that emerged from a number of European monasteries as well. In parts of England that had been under Viking rule, medieval "ghost stories" were recorded by the monks, detailing the horrendous activities of walking cadavers in local communities. Many of these early clerical writers used the term *sanguisuga* to describe such mobile corpses, which seems to imply that they were considered to be blood-drinkers or vampires. The Yorkshire canon, William of Newburgh (1136–1198), for example, accused them in his *Historia Rerum Anglicarum,* of wandering about wrapped in their shrouds, attacking God's servants and of drinking blood. He also charges them with spreading diseases that they brought with them from the grave. Wandering revenants were, according to William, agents of the devil, or were inhabited by a malign spirit that sought to do mankind harm. Such things were wholly evil in William's learned opinion.

Accounts of these malignant revenants or variations of the Viking draugr also appear in a number of other writings from the early medieval period. For example, a Cistercian father, known only as the Monk of Byland, based at the monastic house at Byland in Yorkshire during the 14th century, collected several fragmentary tales in which walking cadavers appear. The monk tells of the revenant of one James Tankerlay, a former rector of Kereby, who despite being a holy man and a cleric, was rather lax in his mortal attitudes and ways. He had procured a number of female concubines and was also reputed to have fathered a number of illegitimate children in his locality. He was laid to rest, according to the monk's account, in the grounds of the chapter house at

Bellelande, but his body refused to remain there. As soon as it was dark, he rose from the grave and began to wander about, traveling as far as Kereby in his nocturnal excursions. Here he went to the house of one of his former concubines and attacked her, gouging out both her eyes until the blood ran. Word of the wandering corpse and its activities soon reached the ears of the Abbot who ordered Tankerlay's coffin to be exhumed and dumped in a nearby swamp at Gormyre.

However, as the coffin was being transported by oxcart, the oxen panicked and fled into the waters of the mire, pulling the cart after them. The two animals involved were almost drowned and had to be rescued. What became of the coffin and the animated corpse is unknown, but they were presumably swallowed up by the marsh. This seemed to bring the incident to an end.

The Abbot's Tale

The monk recounted another story concerning a man who dwelled close to the monastery at Newburgh. This individual may not have been baptized according to recognized religious practice, and although it may not have affected him in life, it meant that he could not lie quiet in the grave. He subsequently rose from his tomb and began to wander around the countryside. He attempted to return to his former home, terrorizing his wife and children, who called upon some neighbors to come and drive him away. Faced with an angry group, the cadaver returned to his tomb, but rose the following night intending to create more mischief. The local people approached the Abbot of Newburgh who instructed one of his monks to stay in the dead man's house for several nights in case the cadaver should return. When the walking corpse did indeed return as soon as it was dark, the monk attacked him and wrestled with him, but was thrown to one side and was injured. (The strength of the dead man

was considerable.) Seeing the holy man's blood, the cadaver became greatly excited and tried to attack him again. Seeing what was happening, several neighbors rushed to the rescue and drove the cadaver away once more. The Abbot, now gravely concerned about the conduct of the revenant, asked that the corpse be exhumed and a Ritual of Absolution be performed over it. When the boy was dug up, it was found that the cerements in which it had been wrapped were badly torn, signifying restlessness in the grave. The ritual, however, seems to have been largely ineffective as, after lying quiet for roughly two or three days, the cadaver was back again, seeking to gain access to his former home and terrifying his family. The matter had now become so serious that it had to be referred to the bishop, who, after much reflection and advisement, instructed that the body be disposed of "in the old way" (that is, dug up, cut to pieces and burned). This was done and, seemingly, the nocturnal nuisance ceased. A similar story is credited to another unnamed churchman known simply as "The Preacher of Ely" (possibly a monk or hermit at one of the monasteries in the marshes of Ely in present-day Cambridgeshire) in a text referred to as *The Book of the Preacher of Ely.* The tale appears as part of a homily on the importance of the observance of the Blessed Sacraments, particularly that of baptism.

German Tales

It was not only in England that such things occurred. In his *Chronicron,* written roughly between 1009 and 1018, Theitmar, the Saxon bishop of Marseburg, Germany, and one of the most venerable writers of the Holy Roman Empire, recounts the tale of a priest in Walseben, Germany, who, just before the town's eventual destruction by the Slavic armies, entered a local church to find it occupied by dead people who had risen from their tombs.

The cadavers greeted him with extreme hostility; a woman whom he knew and who had recently died stepped forward and spitefully told him that he would die of a plague within the year. This prophecy came to pass just as the dead woman had said.

Theitmar recounts a further story in a similar vein that he attributes to Bishop Baudry of the German See of Utrecht. This concerns another priest in the town of Deventer in the Salland region of the Dutch province of Overijssel—the cleric being in charge of a church that had been almost completely rebuilt after its destruction by the Slavs. With the church about to be reconsecrated, the local priest had been charged to oversee the ritual. Arriving there early in the morning, he was amazed to see a congregation of dead people, recently risen from their graves, celebrating Mass, and was even able to hear them singing recognizable psalms. Terrified, he fled the scene and reported the incident to Bishop Baudry, who instructed him to spend the night in the church to ensure that the dead did not desecrate the area. He was also to report back to the bishop what transpired. He did so, but in the middle of the night the very bed on which he was sleeping was thrown out of the building by dead hands. He reported back to the bishop, who told him that he must now go back there, armed with holy relics, and on no account was he to leave the building for which he was in charge.

Although now extremely terrified, the priest did as he was instructed and lay awake in the church until the dead congregation arrived, extremely angry to find him there. They lit a great fire in the aisle of the building, holding him over it and eventually killing him. His charred body was then dumped outside the church as a warning to others. On hearing this, Bishop Baudry ordered a penitential fast to be held for three days to seek succor for the priest's soul. Thietmar concludes that just as the day belongs to the living, so the night belongs to the dead, who are implacably hostile toward their living counterparts.

The risen dead who have not died in a state of grace are corporeal, which means they are able to do harm to the living. This would form the basis of religious opinion for a long time to come.

Forms of the Dead

As the medieval Church consolidated its thinking and dogma, it began to address the problem of the returning dead. Indeed, it could not ignore the question, and a belief in the return from the dead seems to have been well established in the common psyche. Early medieval thought tended to view the phenomenon in two ways. The first was that the souls of the departed might return in a form that the Church referred to as *spiritus.* This form, it was adjudged, constituted the actual *souls* of the deceased, and as such, was insubstantial to the touch and completely subject to God's direct control. These were the stuff of angels and saints, and unusually manifested themselves in singular religious visions and dreams, appearing only to advise, to give succor, and to warn. Sometimes, these spirits became earthbound for one reason or another, and they could manifest themselves as an insubstantial "ghost." They were not to be feared, for the prayers of the faithful or the ordinance of a priest or bishop would help them to move on to the spirit world, where they would do no harm to God's creatures. Indeed, one of the great theologians of the 12th century, Hugh of St. Victor (1096–1141, Prior of the Abbey of St. Victor in Paris) went so far as to consider that these *spiritus* were no more than pure reason—the thoughts and reflections of the godly. Because thoughts and perceptions had no substance, the Prior went on, it was logical that they could do no physical harm or damage property in the material world.

The second form that the returning dead took, however, was far more dangerous. This was the *corpus,* the fleshy husks that the *spiritus* had once

Spiritus Corpus

inhabited, but that were now abandoned. Similar to a deserted house, the empty corpse might prove a dwelling for an unwelcome tenant. An evil spirit that is denied its eternal reward might be forced to return to its former body and reanimate it so that its wickedness might continue; or some unwholesome force might inhabit the discarded husk and animate it in order to fulfill its own dubious purposes or to satisfy its unsavoury lusts. This was considered to be

the basis for the cadavers who were said to wander about the countryside after dark creating mischief and causing harm, which justified the Church's strict approbation of them.

And yet, these definitions were not always so clear-cut, for there were some who argued that certain apparitions (those who returned from the dead) fell somewhere between the two. Sometimes a ghost might have all the attributes of a spiritus, but still be able to attack and injure those whom it encountered like a corpus. Some agreed with Alcher of Clairviaux when, in the 12th century, he followed the Hebrew mystic Isaac of Stella in defining a ghost as "all that is not a body and which, however, is *something* is said rightly to be spirit." The spirit, he went on to argue, is not the body, and yet is in league with the body. Similar to demons, ghosts could continually produce material effects on all that they touched including living beings. Returning corpses, whether they are corpus or spiritus, might have the ability to injure individuals and inflict damage in the living world if they so desired.

Later clerical writers through the early medieval period and into the 14th and 15th centuries carried on the tradition of the corporeal returning dead. Indeed, tales concerning the walking dead began to appear in what came to be known as "court writing" (accounts and stories written by courtiers and churchmen in the courts of the European monarchs), which flourished, especially in England, around this time. Collections of tales—not necessarily ghost stories, but sometimes containing supernatural elements—by writers such as Walter Map, Gervaise of Tilbury, and William of Malmesbury recorded accounts of goblins, werewolves, and the wandering dead in various parts of England, all set in their historical contexts. These were counted as "wonder tales" or "marvels," and were extremely popular at the English court. In his only surviving work, *De Nugis Curialium* (*A Courtier's Trifles*—a collection of stories and anecdotes), Walter Map was careful to draw a clear distinction between the stories of the walking dead that he drew from the countryside and those religious-based stories of earlier times, such as those related by the Monk of Byland. "Not a miracle but a marvel," he wrote. He spoke of fairies (the survivors of an elder race) and unexplained phenomena, such as green-skinned children from a land far beneath the earth. The wandering revenants in his stories however, spread only destruction and disease throughout the countryside, and were symbols of great evil in their own right. This marked a change from the tales of earlier churchmen who had frequently used such tales in order to encourage religious observances. Cadavers now rose from the grave intent on some evil purpose, and their sole function was to cause panic and damage in the communities of the living. William of Newburgh (1136–1198) adopted a somewhat similar theme, no doubt taking up some of Map's former stories and adapting or expanding upon them in his *Historia Rerum Anglicarum* (*History of English Affairs*), as did Gervaise of Tilbury (1157–1234).

As might be expected, the literature produced by these learned men not only served to establish the idea of the walking revenant in the common mind, but also showed a greater level of sophistication than the earlier, more fragmentary tales. These were not simply stories of visions or brief appearances—although some of them are—but served to demonstrate creatures who took on slightly more characteristics (often dangerous ones) than had been previously suggested. Cadavers, revenants, and mobile corpses were now being viewed as agents of the Devil, motivated by some unwholesome force of demon. These were, perhaps, the earliest examples of what we could come to recognize as ghost stories. They would also later lend a greater weight to

similar elements that were imported from other cultures: the vampire and the zombie for example.

Medieval Beliefs

Throughout the early modern period of the 16th and 17th centuries medieval beliefs regarding the returning dead still persisted. Although there were insubstantial and ethereal ghosts that sometimes terrified the living, there were also tales of walking corpses and corporeal revenants that often visited their descendants from time to time. In fact, some of this belief actually fell in with certain Church teachings. Faced with a widespread belief in the returning dead, Church authorities had to come up with some form of dogma to include the ideal. The sprits of the righteous, the clergy said, might return at appointed times, and solely at God's discretion, to their former homes where they might enjoy some of the comforts that they enjoyed when still alive. They might, for example, smoke a pipe of tobacco, eat a meal, or drink a mug of ale; to do this, they needed to have a physical presence about them. They might even complete work that they had left unfinished, or perhaps enjoy the softness of a bed after lying in the cold clay for so long. The clerics also said that the bodies of the truly pure in heart would be incorruptible, so they would appear as they had when they were alive. The times when they might return to the world were clearly designated—usually certain religious feast days and holy days—the most notable of these being the festival of Halloween, which itself was celebrated as a day of the dead. This notion has remained in our minds up to the present day, and Halloween is still considered to be a dark time when the dead may rise and return to places they formerly knew.

If God could resurrect the righteous dead, it seemed logical to Church thinkers that the Devil could also raise those who were not so godly. Evil

people, it was believed, would not rest quietly in their graves, but might become the tools of the enemy of Mankind for his own sinister purposes. Thus, they rose from their tombs, similar to the Viking draugr and wandered about, spreading disease and causing panic and alarm wherever they went. Not only this but, as the agents of Satan's purpose they physically destroyed property and attacked individuals, particularly targeting religious people for their attentions. The faith of the righteous had to be strong enough to deter them, and as the early modern period advanced, these ideas became stronger, firmly establishing the notion of the walking dead in the common consciousness.

Medical History

Yet another strand of the belief came from actual medical history—the condition of *catalepsy,* which might have been more prevalent in earlier societies than we suspect. The condition is characterized by inflexibility of the muscles, rigidity of posture, a low or negligible reaction to pain, and light or shallow breathing. It is believed that it could be brought on by a number of factors, such as trauma or some other medical condition. For all intents and purposes, the sufferer may appear to be dead. However, the condition is not permanent, and the sufferer eventually returns to full sensibility and can resume normal life once more. In past times and to those who were unaware of the condition, this must have appeared as if a dead individual was restored to life. Some of these cataleptics, of course, came back to consciousness within their coffins and perished anyway, but some were restored before burial, causing wonder and terror among their peers. Instances of these conditions were even recorded in parts of England, as late as the 19th century, and one in particular is commemorated in the church where it happened.

Constance Whitney and Other Tales

A unique memorial to a widow named Constance Whitney can be found in the chancel of St. Giles Cripplegate in London. Although Mrs. Whitney died in the late 1800s, an ornamental memorial scroll on the side of her tomb depicts the lady rising from her coffin in the manner of a living corpse. This carving depicts an intriguing, but rather frightening, legend connected with the grave.

Being a woman of some considerable substance, Constance Whitney died and was laid to rest in the tomb clad in all her finery and jewelry. On one of her fingers was a rather fine-looking ring with a large gemstone as its centerpiece. As she was being laid out in her coffin for her various friends to mourn, the greedy church sexton fixed his eye on this ring and resolved to have it for himself as soon as was practicable. He waited until the last of the mourners had departed and the church was clear, approached the coffin that had not been finally sealed, and began to remove the lid. Constance Whitney lay in all her grandeur, and with the valuable ring sparkling on her finger. The sexton attempted to remove it but the lady's knuckles were so swollen (from her arthritis) that it wouldn't budge. Taking out a blade, he started to make a small incision on the finger in order to help the ring move more easily. A small pearl of blood welled up under the band, whereupon Constance Whitney gave a loud sigh and sat up as if she were just waking out of a deep sleep. She had not been dead, but in a cataleptic trance, from which the pain of the sexton's knife had released her. The robbing sexton fled screaming from the church to be arrested by a nearby watchman. Constance Whitney returned to almost full health and lived on for several more years. The uncanny incident, however, was commemorated in her rather bizarre funerary memorial that was erected when she did eventually die.

Constance Whitney

A number of similar tales (some undoubtedly influenced by the original story of Constance Whitney) circulated around the country during this time and often further afield. An extremely similar story is told near Ballycastle, North Antrim, in Northern Ireland, in which a grand lady was buried in the ancient churchyard at Ramoan, just outside the town. Two local ne'er-do-wells exhumed the body, and in an attempt to prize a ring from her finger, the rogues unwillingly revived the lady who sat up in her coffin and asked where she was and what they were doing; by this time the two had fled. Several other such tales are to be found both in parts of Ireland, Wales, and Scotland.

Constance Whitney was not the only person who supposedly "came back" from the dead in Victorian times, as there are accounts of similar instances all across London at the time. A boy named Ernest Wicks (or Wykes), for example, was found lying in Regent's Park, late in 1895, and was assumed to be dead. His body was moved to the Marylebone mortuary, where it was examined by the mortuary keeper prior to the arrival of the official physician. In the course of the examination, the keeper noticed that the chest of the "corpse" was rising and falling almost imperceptibly. He started to rub Ernest's hands and arms, and the boy returned to full consciousness. Upon the arrival of the doctor, he was transferred to the Middlesex hospital where he was pronounced as "recovering from a fit." Following an inquiry in 1902, it emerged that this was not an isolated incident in the child's life, for he had suffered the same experience several times before, and death certificates had been issued by a number of reputable doctors. It seemed that even skilled medical practitioners could be duped by cataleptic fits.

It is quite possible that instances of catalepsy, although not recorded, were just as frequent in earlier periods. If it was possible for trained physicians to mistake the condition for death in the 1800s, then perhaps medical men in the 17th and 18th centuries could make the same mistake. And when, after such a misdiagnosis, the "corpses" may have returned to full health, the idea of the returning corporeal dead was further strengthened in popular belief and imagination. There was also another element that was linked into the mindset: the Resurrectionists.

Resurrectionists

As medicine began to make significant advances in places such as London, Edinburgh, and Dublin (reckoned to be among the foremost medical establishments in the world), the need for doctors and surgeons grew, and many "young men of quality" began to look to the medical profession as a suitable career, and came forward to be trained. The numbers of trainees—particularly in surgical fields—led to a problem. In order to gain knowledge of their profession, trainee surgeons were required to operate on fresh, dead bodies, and these were often in short supply. Hospitals might have been able to procure the bodies of hanged criminals direct from the gallows—indeed under a law dating back to King Henry VIII, English authorities were actually required to deliver a number of executed felons for medical experiments during the course of the year—but quite often these were not wholly suitable. These were men and women who had met their end in a short and violent way, and offered little scope for the examination of, say, the effects of disease on the human frame.

The best way to study such things was to obtain recently buried corpses from graveyards, but of course this was illegal, as it involved the desecration of the dead. Where could hospitals and surgeons obtain their corpses? The answer was that they could buy them from bodysnatchers—individuals with scant regard for the law who would dig up freshly buried corpses at the risk of capture and arrest, and sell them at a substantial profit. In London, Edinburgh, and Dublin, these operative became known as "Resurrectionists" or "Sack-'em-ups." (They carried the bodies in hemp sacks.) Some of them operated individually, others in organized gangs, and some of them made a fairly substantial living out of their dubious and wholly illegal trade. The large surgeries—particularly in London and Edinburgh—paid good money for fresh corpses, and individual surgeons were prepared to "turn a blind eye" as to the source of the cadavers. Even when some of these bodysnatchers turned their hands to a bit of murder in order to obtain freshly dead bodies, the surgeons and hospitals didn't seem to mind. The poor (who died in the London streets from various ailments) usually provided a ready source of interest for surgeons, but so did the rich, because they exhibited more gracious diseases such as gout, which was of considerable interest to certain surgeons. No body apparently was safe from the Resurrectionists' attention.

King of the Corpses

In 19th-century London, "King of the Corpses" was undoubtedly Ben Crouch. The son of a carpenter who sometimes earned his living as a boxer and prize-fighter, Crouch had at one time been a porter in Guy's Hospital, which gave him the contacts and the inclination to be effective in the resurrection trade. More or less abandoning the prize-fighting trade, Crouch turned his attention to grave robbing and made quite a nice living out of it. He began to gather a small gang around him: Bill Harnett and his brother Jack, who hated Crouch and his vicious ways, but nevertheless stuck with him; Tom Light, a person of "low intellect," who was arrested for wheeling a dead body on a barrow in broad daylight; Joseph Napier, a former seaman who worked as a grave digger in the Spa Fields in Clerkenwell (a useful member to have in the gang); along with several others. Ben Crouch was a dandy, sly, and vicious bully, but this didn't stop the surgeons at the various hospitals from dealing with him. And the trade paid enough for Crouch to dress in the finest clothes and strut around parts of London as if he owned the city. For many years, he and his gang remained among the foremost bodysnatchers in London, matched only by their great rivals, the Saffron Hill gang led by Israel Chapman.

Bodysnatchers

The bodysnatching season usually began in autumn, because the dark nights began to draw in. The bodysnatching trade needed the cover of darkness because the Resurrectionists worked by the light of shielded lanterns and candles that were placed in glass jars to cut down on the light, so they did not draw attention to themselves. It was also the time when the new terms were starting in hospital anatomy schools and surgeons were in need of fresh corpses. Bodysnatchers such as Crouch would present themselves at the surgeon's office and begin to "take orders" for the coming months. Their clients were not common doctors, for Crouch would have counted many of the prominent surgeons and anatomists of the day as his clients. Among them were Sir Charles Bell, Sir Joshua Brooks of the prestigious Blenheim Street surgeries, and John Taunton, founder of the London Truss Society. Although they disliked Crouch, these surgeons knew that he had a reputation for "delivering the goods," and were prepared to work with him and his like.

Many of the Resurrectionsts, including both the Crouch and Saffron Hill gangs, drew their "commodities" from the churchyard of Christchurch in Spitalfields. Indeed, so widespread were the instances of resurrections in that area that many people were actually afraid to be buried there because they

did not want their remains to be desecrated. An example of the place's reputation is shown in the late 1700s when 73-year-old Mary Mason was buried at Christ Church in a coffin that was covered in bands of lead and secured with a padlock, in order to avoid the attentions of the Resurrectionists. Other families either employed watchmen or stood guard themselves to keep watch over the graves of their loved ones, lest their bodies be dug up and transported away for medical dissection. It was not only in London cemeteries that this occurred but also at other churches throughout the country. Many local authorities permitted such vigils to last for several weeks or more, because, after a certain period of time, the body was considered to be beyond use for dissection purposes. When there were fewer burials, Crouch and his associates usually resorted to murder without too much difficulty.

Around the same time that Ben Crouch and Israel Chapman were operating in London, Irish bodysnatchers were also serving the needs of the College of Surgeons in Dublin. Most famous of the Irish Resurrectionists was the eccentric George "Crazy Crow" Hendrick, who served several terms in jail for his nocturnal activities. Crazy Crow was a wild-looking, violent, and extremely drunken character who, unlike the dapper Ben Crouch, had no illusions about his social status or appearance. He took to distributing copies of his picture together with an unflattering poem that he probably composed himself:

With a look ferocious and with beer replete,
See Crazy Crow beneath his minstrel weight,
His voice as frightful as great Etna's roar,
Which spreads its horrors to the distant shore.

Equally hideous is his well-known face,
Murders each ear till whiskey makes it cease.

Crazy Crow's favorite hunting ground in Dublin City was St. Andrew's Church, where his disheveled form appeared out of the gloom after a funeral had finished, giving late mourners a fright. It was his custom to hang around such burying grounds like a ghastly phantom until it was dark, and then began his grisly and nefarious trade. In many respects, he resembled nothing more than a graveyard ghost, and legends of his exploits frequently haunted the pages of the Dublin newspapers. In 1825 he was arrested and thrown into jail, making the front page of most of the Dublin broadsheets—it did not discourage him, but made him all the more determined to continue with his dubious trade; on his release he was back in St. Andrew's again. Similar to Ben Crouch in London he worked from time to time as a hospital porter, and this may have guided him toward the corpses that he supplied to the surgeons. Later, when the 1832 Anatomy Act became a law, he gave up bodysnatching and became a maker of musical instruments—an occupation at which he finished his days. The Anatomy Act of Parliament stated that all anatomy schools must be licensed by the British Home Secretary under very strict guidelines, thus limiting some of the Resurrectionists' clientele.

Although Crazy Crow was a bizarre and extremely eerie character, he was not the only such individual pursuing a ghastly trade along the Dublin streets. Of equal notoriety was "Billy-in-the-Basin," a legless invalid who propelled himself around in a great metal basin or bath. Although a dwarf, Billy was believed to have prodigious strength, particularly in his arms. He was also considered to be extremely sly and resourceful, and he was remarkably adept at covering his tracks. This is why no definite location in Dublin is given for

many of his activities; some say he worked in the alleyways off what is now Grafton Street near the City Centre, and others say he worked on Earl Street just off Sackville Street (now O'Connell Street). His modus operandi was always been the same: He would appear as a legless beggar in his basin asking for money in some dark entry. When some kindly soul would stop, Billy would claim to have some secret to impart if only the person would stoop down. When he did so, Billy would grab the victim's neck in his powerful hands and break it. Like a predatory animal, he would drag the dead body into his alleyway, where he would rob it and later give it to the Resurrectionists.

Similar to their English counterparts, Dublin surgeons were not extremely particular about where they obtained the dead bodies for their anatomy lessons, and were quite willing to deal with the Resurrectionists and murderers if they could guarantee a steady supply of cadavers. They had no qualms about dealing with the likes of Crazy Crow or Billy-in-the-Basin. One of the most prominent Dublin surgeons of his day, Dr. Samuel Clossey, who reputedly operated a college of anatomy in Dublin between 1786 and 1803, was said to have obtained "stiffs" from every part of the city for his surgery.

Around 1828 a rather scurrilous newssheet, detailing the activities and exploits of some of the more colorful bodysnatchers, began to circulate throughout Dublin. It claimed the "Wonderful Discovery of Barbarous Assassins Who Stop Live Children and Bleed them to Death." The printer was a disreputable character known as Munster Jack (John Cramer) who operated a primitive printing press in Walker's Alley. In a crudely printed publication, he recounted tales of half-dead children—near corpses—found wandering the streets after escaping from Resurrectionists who had assaulted them with sharp blades in order to drag them away and sell their bodies for medical science. Using the same printing press, Munster Jack also circulated a crude pamphlet

Burke and Hare

concerning the horrendous activities of people such as Crazy Crow, Billy-in-the-Basin, and earlier Dublin Resurrectionists such as Richard Fox. This, together with reports from some Dublin newspapers, kept the notion of cadavers being taken from (or emerging from) their graves.

But perhaps it was Edinburgh that became most closely associated with the bodysnatching trade. Scottish surgeons enjoyed an unenviable reputation in the early medical world, and consequently their schools of anatomy and dissection were always well subscribed with eager students anxious to learn from them. The demand for cadavers for these establishments was therefore extremely high. Instances of grave robbery and infant murder were regularly reported in the newspapers all across Edinburgh. Around 1752, two women, Jean Waldie and Helen Torrance, were hanged in the city's Grassmarket section for the murder of a 7-year-old boy with the intent of selling his body for dissection. His price would have been 3 shillings. Although charged with this particular murder, it was certainly not the first such outrage that both women had committed, and stories of their crimes were spread all through the city, towns, and villages beyond.

However, the most famous Edinburgh bodysnatchers were two Irishmen, William Burke and William Hare, whose names became known far and wide beyond the city. Between the years 1827 and 1828 (five or so years before the Anatomy Act put an end to such practices) Burke and Hare, together with Helen MacDougall and Hare's wife, Margaret, made a lucrative living selling bodies to the Edinburgh surgeons at high prices. It is not clear whether the two men had known each other for a long period—perhaps they'd known each other as laborers through working on the Union Canal (also known as the Edinburgh and Glasgow Union Canal)—but when Burke came to stay in Hare's lodging house they certainly struck up a friendship and a grisly business partnership.

Their first criminal exploit was to sell the body of an elderly soldier and military pensioner named Donald who also lodged in Hare's rooming house. He suddenly died, owing his landlord 4 pounds rent. In order to recoup this money, Hare sold the body for dissection to a local anatomy school with Burke's help. This gave both men a taste for the bodysnatching trade, and in November 1828, they managed to remove a cadaver from its coffin and sold it to the Edinburgh Medical School for around 7 pounds, which was a good sum in those days. The transaction also brought them first into contact with the celebrated surgeon Dr. Robert Knox, who would become one of their most regular clients. Shortly after, one of Hare's other tenants, known as Joseph the Miller, took ill, and although he was not as ill as Donald had been, the scheming landlord resolved to do away with him—Joseph was already behind on his rent and was worth more dead than alive. Hare discussed the matter with Burke, who had served at one time in the Donegal militia (although probably only as a servant to an officer) and professed himself "quite handy" at doing away with people. Between them, they hatched a plan and, after Hare had plied the unfortunate Joseph with whiskey, Burke overpowered him and smothered him; they then sold his body to the anatomists.

In February 1828, Margaret Hare persuaded an elderly pensioner named Abigail Simpson to spend the evening in their home. Having plied the woman with a strong drink, Burke and Hare then did away with her, selling her body on to Robert Knox, who remarked on the "good quality" of the body and paid them 10 pounds. Shortly after, Burke brought two prostitutes—Mary Paterson and Janet Brown—back to the house for "an evening's frivolity." Brown left shortly after following a disagreement over money, but Paterson stayed on and was subsequently killed. Her body was so fresh when it was sold on that Knox paid a staggering 15 pounds for it. However, the enterprise was a risky one, for

some members of the anatomy students had consorted with the prostitute themselves not long before and recognized her body on the anatomy slab in front of them. There was now a suspicion as to what was happening, although Knox managed to keep things quiet.

Spurred on by the money that they were making, Burke and Hare grew ever bolder and now resorted to murder in order to obtain "remarkably fresh" corpses. Burke had assumed the more respectable job of cobbler (an occupation at which he displayed a little skill) but in reality the trade brought him into contact with a number of people who could be useful to him in other ways—as cadavers. One of these was an elderly beggar-woman named Effie, from whom he sometimes bought strips of leather for his work, who was in rather poor health, but still able to go about. She had no immediate family and, in that respect, looked like an eminently suitable candidate for the attentions of Burke and Hare, because nobody would question her disappearance. He invited Effie to come out drinking with him, and, when she was well inebriated, he killed her, and both he and Hare sold her body to Knox for 10 pounds.

On their way home in the summer of 1828, the pair came upon two policemen carrying a drunk man between them. The officers told Burke that they were carrying the man home, having found him outside a public house, and asked if he knew where the inebriate lived. Burke replied that he knew him well, and if the officers would give him to them both he and Hare would see that he got home. The officers were happy enough to do this, whereupon Burke and Hare took him into a courtyard and murdered him, placing his body in a herring cart for transportation to the Edinburgh Medical School.

Later, Burke would meet another drunken man whom he began to lure back to his lodgings with promises of whiskey. On the way there, however, an elderly lady and her grandson stopped them—a child of about 5 or 6 years

old—who needed directions. Burke immediately abandoned the old man and promised to personally escort the pair to the place they wished to go. First, however, he would offer them some "refreshments" at his own home. While Helen and Margaret looked after the child, Burke and Hare took the old woman into the back of the house where they plied her with whiskey; when she was suitably intoxicated they killed her by smothering her. However, there was a problem with the boy, who had become incredibly fretful about the absence of his grandmother, and, he refused to take any of the whiskey that was offered to him. Burke then invited the child to come and see his grandmother in the back of the house, and when he got him there, he broke the youngster's back across his knee, killing him instantly. Both bodies were put in wooden barrels and later transported to Knox. Together both bodies fetched a sum of 8 pounds.

At this time, the murderers apparently split up, with Burke and Helen MacDougal moving out of Hare's rooming house to some premises nearby. The cause of this was reputed to be that Hare wanted Helen MacDougal dead and that he and Margaret had plotted her murder. They had approached Burke, who was against the idea, and had warned MacDougal. However, once they had moved, the two "sack-'em-ups" returned to the old ways once more with all differences seemingly forgotten. However, their luck was starting to run out.

Burke and Hare's arrogance started to raise suspicions in their direction. They had been extremely fortunate in the murder of Mary Paterson, whose body had been recognized (Knox had covered for them), but there had been some whispers among the students and there was still talk of involving the police. The murderers paid no attention, and their next victim was even more well known.

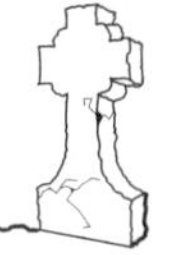

Eighteen-year-old James Wilson, or "Daft Jamie," as he was known, was a simple soul—slow in his ways but kindly—and something of a character in Edinburgh's West Port area. He was a particular favorite of many young children, who often gathered around him to hear his stories and riddles. Although he lived among kindly folk who often gave him a bed for the night, he had a widowed mother who lived close to the West Port area and whom he visited regularly. He had few possessions—simply a snuffbox and spoon. The box had seven holes in it by which the boy was able to tell the days of the week. In October 1828, Jamie ran into William Hare, whom he vaguely knew, and engaged in conversation. Daft Jamie was looking for a bed for the night, and Hare agreed "out of kindness" to let him lodge for the night in his lodging house. Delighted, Jamie accompanied him home, where Margaret prepared him a meal.

From a nearby public house Burke watched the proceedings and then made his way over to the house. Burke and Hare tried to persuade the boy to have some whiskey in order to get him intoxicated before they murdered him. Jamie took a few sips, said that he didn't like and would take no more. However, he'd taken enough and was soon dozing fitfully, whereupon Burke began to strangle him. Jamie woke up and, being stronger than he looked, wrested with Burke, pinning him to the wall. Answering his partner's screams for help, Hare came in, and together he and Burke overpowered and smothered Daft Jamie. They then took his body to Knox, who gave them 5 pounds for it. Jamie was so well known, even to the medical students of Edinburgh, that whenever the cadaver was uncovered, he was recognized immediately. Knox, who was the anatomist, denied it, but the identity was proven by a deformity of the right foot. Knox nevertheless proceeded, with undue haste, to the dissection, and hoped that the matter had dropped. However, Jamie's mother showed up and went directly to the Edinburgh police in order to find out what had happened to her son. There were some investigations—the murder of Daft Jamie was not a high-profile case as far as the police were concerned—and several people recalled how they had seen the boy with William Hare, although Hare himself was never questioned. Nevertheless, it turned the eyes of the law to the grisly pair; they were now under police suspicion.

The last murder occurred only a few weeks afterward—on Halloween in 1828. While drinking in a public house, Burke met up with an elderly Irish woman named Mary Docherty who looked as if she might be a candidate for the medical school. Mary Docherty said she came from Donegal, and Burke claimed to come from the country as well. He also falsely claimed that his mother's maiden name had also been Docherty. Believing him to be a fellow countryman and perhaps even a relative, Mary Docherty agreed to go home with him to have a few drinks and celebrate Halloween.

Back at his house, the lady was well received by Helen MacDougal and by James and Ann Gray, who were at that time lodging with Burke. As the evening wore on, Burke persuaded Mary to stay the night and asked the Grays if they would mind spending the night over at William Hare's, which they readily did, but were told to return for breakfast in the morning.

The carousing and whiskey-drinking at Burke's house continued until well after midnight, but in the early hours of the morning, a man passing by the dwelling heard a woman screaming and shouting "murder!" several times. He ran to fetch a policeman but, finding none in the surrounding streets, he returned to find the house quiet. Assuming that he might have imagined it or that it was simply an argument that had now subsided, he went on about his business.

In the morning, the Grays returned to find Mary Docherty gone. Burke told them that she had left early that morning, which they found odd, because she had departed without saying goodbye. However, when Ann Gray went up to their room to fetch some woollen stockings, Burke ran after her and persuaded her not to go—he would fetch them himself. Similarly when she went past the back staircase to fetch some potatoes, Burke lingered at the foot of the steps. When he was gone, Ann slipped up and peered into their bedroom. In the bed she saw the body of an old woman whom she believed to be Mary Docherty, lying half-covered by blankets. She went down and confronted Helen MacDougal, who begged her not to say anything, because the body was worth 10 pounds to her and her partner, and she offered to share the money with the Grays. Ann was not convinced and revealed what she had seen to her husband James, who was outraged by MacDougal's confession. The couple went to the police and informed them of what they knew.

By the time the constables arrived, however, the bed in the back room was empty. Two men, later identified as Burke and Hare, had been seen leaving the premises carrying a large tea chest between them. The police immediately took Burke and MacDougal into custody for questioning. Almost immediately a discrepancy began to emerge in their stories, although presumably both had compared notes. Burke said that Mary Docherty had left at 7 a.m., after spending the night in his house, whereas Helen MacDougal confidently stated that she had left at seven o'clock the previous evening and had not spent the night with them at all. This 12-hour discrepancy was enough to arouse police suspicions and they questioned the couple further. They also received a tipoff that took them to Dr. Robert Knox's anatomy rooms, where they found the body of Mary Docherty stretched out on a table. Knox himself was unable to explain how it had got there, but, being an eminent surgeon, he was never charged—even as an accomplice.

Faced with this admittedly circumstantial evidence, the stories of Burke and MacDougal began to unravel. MacDougal claimed that she had never even met Mary Docherty, even though the Grays testified that they had seen the two women together; Burke claimed that a stranger (whom he later named as William Hare) had called with him to have boots mended and had been carrying a large tea chest. Hare was also brought in, and he seemed so nervous that the authorities were sure he was concealing something. Besides, his detention had begun to throw up a number of stories—how he had been seen with Daft Jamie Wilson and a couple of others who had disappeared. Moreover, some women's clothing had been found at his house that clearly didn't belong to his wife. At this point, the prostitute Janet Brown came forward and identified them as belonging to Mary Paterson who had finished up on the anatomists' table.

Hare told police that Burke was the leader of the two men, and Hare was told that if he provided evidence and implicated Burke, he would receive a pardon. This he did, and Burke and Helen MacDougal were brought to trial at the end of 1828. Burke was found guilty, but MacDougal was released under the unique Scottish verdict of "not proven." William Burke went to the scaffold in Edinburgh on January 28, 1829. By then most of the citizens of Edinburgh knew of his crimes, and the names Burke and Hare had passed into popular folklore. Many of those who had come to see him hang called for Hare and Dr. Robert Knox to join him on the scaffold.

William Hare himself was released from prison, where he'd been detained for his own safety, and eventually disappeared. He did not attempt to join his wife Margaret who may have fled to Ireland; Helen MacDougall, it was believed, took passage to Australia to avoid the wrath of the various mobs that regularly attacked Burke's house. One story states that Hare was blinded by a mob in Carlisle (where he was last seen) and was finally reduced to begging on the streets of London. Dr. Robert Knox continued to lecture in anatomy, but

he had been ruined by the scandal. Gradually, his classes began to diminish and he was the object of abuse by mobs. He was forced to apply for a post in the medical school, but was unsuccessful. He finished his days as a general doctor in a London hospital before dying in 1862.

The case of Burke and Hare became famous throughout Scotland, and, thanks to the printing presses, word of it even reached the shores of America. Writers painted the most lurid pictures of the two, often giving false or misleading accounts of their crimes. Some pamphlets that circulated shortly after Burke's trial spoke of "half-strangled corpses" rising from the dissection table to the horror of the surgeons and onlookers. Others spoke of the Resurrectionists being surprised and terrified when the corpses they were seeking to exhume rose up in front of them in the style of Mrs. Constance Whitney, mentioned earlier. One pamphlet—*The Terrible but Wonderful Revelation of the Crimes of the Resurrectionists Burke and Hare and Many Others*—probably published anonymously some time in the 1830s, spoke of revived "corpses" rising from their coffins in dramatic style in order to thwart the best attempts of the sack-'em-ups. None of these accounts bore even the slightest scintilla of truth, but were generally accepted by most people. Burke and Hare were styled as "ghouls," and even became equated with the corpses that they were said to "resurrect." Their murders began to assume less importance than their ghostly reputations. Indeed, an old Edinburgh children's skipping song of uncertain date and origin served to keep their names alive and linked them to Dr. Robert Knox:

Up the close and down the stair,
But an' ben wi' Burke and Hare,
Burke's the butcher, Hare's the thief,
Knox is the boy that buys the beef.

American Grave-Robbing

In America, too, grave robbing had been implanted in the colonial consciousness. As early as 1655, a court in Rhode Island passed a law that stated: "If any person shall be accused of robbing any, if ye Corte (sic) shall be satisfied of ye probation of it, ye party or parties shall be fined or suffer corporall punishment or both." The reason for digging up bodies in colonial America was, however, slightly different from that in the United Kingdom. There were no great anatomy schools in the early Colonies to which the Resurrectionists could sell the corpses, but there were other people: black magicians. This was demonstrated when, in 1662, the Massachusetts Assembly passed "An Act against Conjuration, Witchcraft, and Dealing with Evil and Wicked Spirits." It included a section providing the death penalty for any person who "shall take up any dead man, woman or child out of his or her grave or any other place where the dead body resteth or the skin or bone or any other part of a dead person to be used in any manner of witchcraft, sorcery, charm or enchantment." This was a response against a perceived growth of witchcraft in the colonies following the alleged outbreak at Salem. There was, however, a strong belief that elements from dead bodies could be used for necromantic practices—the summoning of evil spirits to inhabit cadavers and reanimate them with a kind of pseudo-life.

An anonymous pamphlet dated around the late 1670s, supposedly printed in Boston and entitled "*A Wonderful Discoverie of Doubtful Magicks in the Village of Ipswich or The Heathen's Purpose Discover'd* relates how Robert Rudd of Ipswich Village, Massachusetts, enlisted the aid on a "heathenish Indian conjurer" in order to restore life to his wife, who had predeceased him. Using a powder made from crushed human remains and Indian magic,

he revived the woman "but briefly and without her wits," but was brought before the courts for taking part in an act of witchcraft. Although he was found guilty, he was not executed, but rather confined to prison for a time "because he was old and had previously been of a good Christian character as many attested. And because he had been misled by an Indian." Such stories would place the idea of the walking dead—in particular the Haitian zombie—at the forefront of American thinking and imagination.

Even up until the 20th century, the idea of "goofer dust," made from the powdered remains of long-dead corpses, was common in many forms of American hill and mountain magic. It was said that the dust, which could be purchased from mountain wizards and granny women, could cure most ailments and restore the dead to life. This is a central theme in a series of pamphlets attributed to John George Hohman, who also wrote *Der Lange Verborgene Freunde* (*The Long Lost Friend,* published in Pennsylvania in 1820), a celebrated compendium of mountain magic, pow-wows, and hoodoos. In the realms of hill sorcery, the dead, it seemed, could also raise the dead.

Although it is true to say that early America did not boast anatomical schools on the grandiose level of Edinburgh with whom grave-robbers could trade their grisly wares, this didn't mean that there were not prominent anatomists in a later period. William Shippen, Jr., of Philadelphia, Pennsylvania, for example, had studied under the celebrated English surgeon John Hunter; when he returned home in 1762, he instituted anatomical classes and lectures that continued until the Revolution in 1777. Similar to some of his predecessors Thomas Cadwalader, also in Philadelphia (1750), and John Bard and Peter Middleton in New York (1752), he drew his supply of corpses from the numbers of dead Indians who had been executed for various "crimes," such as defending their property.

However, Shippen's supply was sporadic, and often ran out; there was a suspicion that he was obtaining fresh supplies by digging them up from the Potter's Field (a burying ground for the poor and destitute, and for those who had been infected with disease). His dissecting rooms were attacked several times by mobs that stoned the windows; when he went out his carriage was the target of a number of projectiles including several musket balls. However, nothing against him could be proven. Similar treatment was meted out to Dr. Jonathan Knight, who was the first professor of anatomy and physiology at the medical institution of Yale College. Knight had kept the body of a young woman in his cellar, lightly covered in soil and presumably for anatomical purposes. According to two letters written by the town constable, Erastus Osborn, following a search of Knight's surgery in January 1824, the girl's body had been found resting under a flagstone in the cellar in a hole that was about 3 feet deep and 2 feet in diameter. Knight quickly blamed one of his students, Ephria Colborn, basing his accusation on some gossip that he'd heard among the college assistants. Colborn was later arrested, charged, and convicted of grave robbery for the purposes of anatomical research. He was sentenced to nine months in jail with a fine of 300 pounds.

Although America never boasted the same organized bodysnatching that characterized the likes of Edinburgh and London, individual occurrences were to be found throughout several states from the early 1800s onward. The Revolutionary War had given up enough bodies, but even that bounteous supply was not inexhaustible. And although there were no established criminals gangs in the style of Ben Crouch or Israel Chapman, there were nevertheless groups of individuals who sporadically raided graves and raised the dead for their own purposes. In 1770, for example, a group of Harvard students founded the Anatomical Society and the Spunker Club; the objectives of the latter were to secure bodies for anatomical dissection by any available means. Their main client seems to have been a Professor Church, a lecturer in anatomy at Harvard.

And the idea of corpses in the use of black magic had not gone away either, even in the mid-19th century. In 1852, for instance, a ramshackle cabin, sometimes bearing the misspelled sign "Chemical Labaratary," was to be found along the road that led from Cincinnati to Walnut Hills in Ohio. Locals tended to stay away from the place, and, when the police eventually raided the shack in response to complaints late in the year, they found that it had been used as a kind of a "factory" for the "preparation" of dead bodies and skeletons. In fact, parts from roughly 20 bodies were found—being used in the preparation of "goomer" (witchcraft) charms to relieve sickness or cast curses. Others were being sold to anatomists in Cincinnati itself. Although the hut itself was deserted (the inhabitants having fled), a number of dark robes and cloaks were found, and a number of "strange books" were also discovered, which in the eyes of Puritan Ohio were counted as "devil work." It is not clear as to whether anybody was actually arrested for it, but the incident certainly gave Ohio anatomists an extremely bad name.

Indeed, of all the states, Ohio seems to have been a particularly fertile ground for certain Resurrectionists. This was largely due to the activities of one particular individual: the colorfully named "Old Cunny," an Irishman of somewhat dubious ancestry. He made a moderate living selling freshly "resurrected" bodies to the Ohio Medical College. An extremely vindictive person, when some of the students played a trick on him, he slipped them a corpse that had died from smallpox, managing to fatally infect two or three of them with the disease.

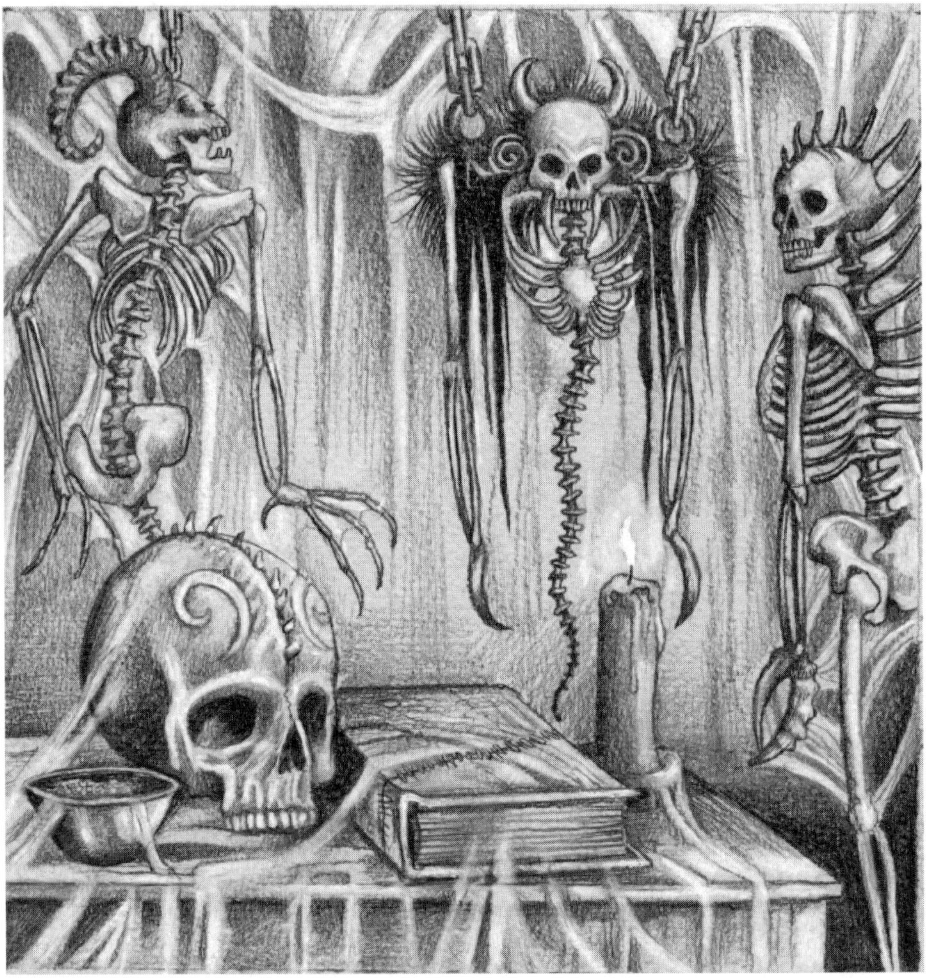

Goomer Charms

Indeed, as the looting of individual graves increased slightly in the later 1800s, some rural communities and the families of deceased employed armed guards to keep watch near the graves of the recently departed. This followed a pattern that had already been established in the Old Countries, and reflected

some of the horror with which ordinary people viewed the nocturnal activities of some of these "ghouls." The atrocities of Resurrectionist Roderick Clow in Hoosick, New York, who sold his bodies to Dr. P.M. Armstrong, a noted dissectionist, prompted the relatives of Ruth Sharague (died 1846) to pen the following verses that later appeared on her tombstone:

Her body stolen by fiendish men,
Her bones anatomised,
Her soul we trust has risen to God,
Where few physicians rise

The notion of Resurrectionists formed a powerful figure in the psyche of the mid- to late-19th century, nearly everywhere in the West, even sporadically appearing in the literature of the period. The father of Jerry Cruncher for instance, who appears in Charles Dickens's *A Tale of Two Cities* dabbles in the gruesome business, as does Jerry himself, whereas the poet Robert Southey (1774–1843) refers to the practice in his poem "The Surgeon's Warning." He even goes into some detail on the activities of the sack-'em-ups and the money that they could command. But the greatest and most popular work on the subject came from the pen of Robert Louis Stevenson whose celebrated short story *The Body Snatchers* was a thinly veiled reference to the activities of Burke and Hare, and, Dr. Robert Knox in particular. The story became established in the minds of many readers, and the idea of corpses being torn from their graves or rising from some cataleptic trance sent a thrill of horror through the 19th-century mind. Add to this a widely read article that appeared in the *London Magazine* in 1827, attributed to a certain "L.R.," which was entitled "The Pleasures of Body Snatching," and the idea of the resurrected corpse was well emblazoned on the public mind. But there were other strands that made up the image of the returning corpse as well—among them were the half-hanged.

The Half-Hanged

Death by hanging was usually caused by the breaking of an individual's neck after a sudden drop—in most circumstances using a rope noose tied about the throat. In some instances, however, and for one reason or another, the neck did not break, and the person was slowly strangled or suffocated to death. Sometimes the hanging failed altogether, and the individual was cut down still more or less alive. Because the sentence had been carried out, the failed hanging was counted as an "act of God"; these people could not be re-hanged unless they or their families actually requested it. In medieval and early modern times, some hangmen pulled the legs of the hanging corpse to ensure that the neck broke immediately, but, as the law became more formalized (particularly in England), these men could have been charged with murder, so few attempted this merciful action. Those who were cut down were known as the "half-hanged," and there were more of them than might be imagined. But escaping the rope in such a manner was perhaps not as great a fortune as it seemed. In many cases, the blood supply to the brain had been interrupted by near strangulation, and a good number of those who were cut down were left mentally incapable, unable to resume normal lives. In the majority of cases, they had to be cared for, and, as one writer pointed out, it would have been far better for them had they actually been executed. The word *half-hanged* became a term of abuse or ridicule, denoting that the person concerned was mentally incompetent or had limited faculties.

In fact there were even a number of ribald songs, sung in public houses and taverns, concerning the half-hanged. For example, in 1728, Margaret Dixon

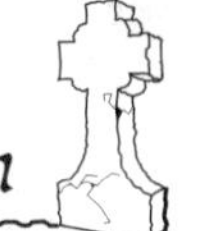

was hanged in Edinburgh's Grassmarket for the murder of her own child. The body was cut down and placed on a cart, which was then driven over the cobbled streets on the way to the mortuary. Halfway there, the hangman and the carter stopped at a tavern for a drink, and although they were inside having a refreshment, the "corpse" sat up to the astonishment and terror of those around. The jogging and bumping of the cart seemed to have revived Margaret, who had not been completely dead. She was taken home and after a few days had made an almost full recovery, although she was never quite the same. Her husband, however, had been declared a widower at the time of her execution and the two were forced, under Scottish law, to remarry. This story was the catalyst to a number of rather bawdy but extremely popular songs all across Scotland and beyond concerning "half-hangit Maggie Dixon" or "Half Hangit Meg." But the notion of the hanged corpse rising from the mortuary cart had nevertheless left a terrified mark on the consciousness of the Edinburgh population. Nor was Margaret Dixon the only one of the "half-hanged" to be so celebrated.

In 1736, two murderers, Vernham and Harding, were publicly hanged at St. Michael's Hill in Bristol. When cut down, both were found to be still alive. Vernham was taken to the house of a local surgeon, where he revived, rubbed his knees, and shook hands with several of those in attendance. He did not linger long, however, but died before the day was out. His partner, Joshua Harding, however, was also revived and remained in reasonable health for a number of years, becoming known as "Half-Hanged Harding." He remained in the local Bridewell Prison where he became an object of curiosity, receiving many visitors, some of whom gave him money. But, similar to Maggie Dixon, he too was the victim of scurrilous and ribald rhyme.

This ribaldry may well have affected the decisions of another such character: the celebrated Irish murderer Half-Hanged McNaghten. His real name was John McNaghten, but in 1752 he was convicted of murdering his former sweetheart Mary-Anne Knox. When the rope broke at his execution in Lifford, he called for a fresh one. "I will never be known as Half-Hanged McNaghten" he declared, which, ironically, he was.

America, too, had its own versions and poems of the "half-hanged." In the 1680s, Mary Webster was hanged near Salem, Massachusetts, on a charge of witchcraft, predating the famous Salem witch trials. When cut down, she was still alive, and, although she seems to vanish from the pages of history, her name lived on in an old American ballad called "Half-Hanged Mary."

The notion of executed corpses rising again spread a kind of fearful interest all through 18th- and 19th-century societies. Indeed, the sight of Margaret Dixon rising from the mortuary cart had created panic in all those who saw it, and the event was celebrated long after she had actually died. This was perhaps linked in folklore to the ancient medieval ideas of the Viking draugr and other such horrors in the public mind, and kept the notion of the walking dead very much to the fore. Coupled with this were some of the religious notions current at the time.

Calling of the Dead

In the religious fervour that characterized the era from 1730 to 1740, in what became known as "The First Great Awakening" on the American east coast, there was much debate about the status of those who had "died in Christ." There was a persistent conviction—not only in America but in Europe as well—that mankind was living in the "End Times," and that Christ would soon return to call the faithful to Paradise. But what would be the state of the bodies? The debate raged for many years, and seemed to be brought into a sharper focus following the Dark Day on May 19, 1780, when the entire east coast of America witnessed a solar eclipse. This was taken as incontrovertible proof that the end of the world was fast approaching. However, slightly before this event, some of the more eccentric religious groups had taken steps to ensure that when Christ arrived, they were there in physical body to greet him.

One of these groups was the followers of Shadrack Ireland—a bizarre preacher who had originally been a follower of the early Methodist George Whitefield. However, in the 1760s, he formed his own church, and the members were known as the Perfectionists. Sometimes described as a Baptist, sometimes as a Primitive Methodist, Ireland preached that the bodies of the "saints" (the Godly) were incorruptible, and that even after death they would not decay. Consequently on the Last Great Day, Christ would expect his followers to rise, whole and undecayed from their graves, to join him. He did not, Ireland taught, expect the righteous to claw their way through grave earth in order to answer the last trumpet, and so Perfectionist followers began to construct great stone-lined chambers under the New England hills, in which stone slabs were placed for the dead to lie upon while they waited for the call. His message was taken up by other smaller groups who did something similar. The idea of uncorrupted, unshrouded, and un-coffined bodies lying beneath the hills, ready to rise must have prayed on early American minds even after Ireland and his followers were long gone, because following his death, many of them joined Mother Ann Lee's Shakers.

All of these strands—the medieval notions of the violent risen dead, the later activities of the Resurrectionists, the half-hanged, and the holy corpses awaiting the Final Call—came together in the human psyche to create a notion of the dead who were "merely sleeping" and might rise from their tombs and walk about at any time, for whatever purpose. There was now only one more element needed to complete the picture, and that came from ancient Egypt.

Egyptian Hangings

Similar to many other ancient peoples the Egyptians did not view death as the end of all things. Certainly it marked the termination of physical involvement in this world, but beyond the tomb the body could be renewed and continue to live very much as it had in this world. In order for the renewal process to take place, the body had to descend into the Underworld—a realm known as Nun—where it would be submerged in the primal waters, reemerging to begin a new life beyond death. In order for this to happen, the body had to be preserved intact. Therefore, the ancient Egyptians mummified their dead by drying the cadavers out, coating them in natron (a sodium-based element that aided the "drying out" process and that prevented bacteria from forming in the organs together with preservative gums, and wrapping them in bandages before placing them in their tombs in preparation for the next world. This was an incredibly expensive process, and in many cases it was the rich, noble classes who embraced mummification in a wholesale way—especially the Pharaohs or rulers of Egypt who believed that they would come back as incarnations of the god Osiris and therefore needed to be whole in body. Although the Egyptians were not the only ancient people to mummify their dead—the Chinchorro races of the Peru/Chile border in South America had been doing something similar from about 5000 BCE—they are unquestionably the best known, largely through much publicized excavations of their tombs.

Although Egyptology—the study of Egyptian antiquities and relics with reference to both Egyptian history and archaeology—had been considered a science since the early 19th century, it was during the early 20th that it really came to prominence in the Western mind.

On the western bank of the Nile, just across from the ancient capital of Thebes (modern-day Luxor), lay a large valley system known as the Valley of the Kings. Wadi Biban el-Muluk, or Gate of Kings, signified a portal into the other world through which Pharaohs might pass. This was a vast necropolis in which many of the ancient kings of Egypt were laid to rest. In fact most of the Egyptian pharaohs who reigned over Egypt following the fall of the Hyksos (a group of foreign rulers who controlled the Middle Kingdom for 108 years in the 17th century BCE are interred there, many of them in great splendor.

In the late 18th and 19th centuries, many explorers and archaeologists were drawn to the Valley, lured there by stories of fabulous treasures that had been allegedly buried with the dead monarchs (although this was not always the case). In order to protect the Valley and its tombs, many rumors were spread. The most prominent was that many of the tombs were cursed, and that those who attempted to break into them would meet a horrible end. This was the "Curse of the Pharaohs," a supernatural retribution on all of those who dared defile the sacred burial sites. And the idea of a bandaged, shrouded dead body fitted in well with that. Similar to the ancient Viking draugr, the swathed mummy would rise from its sarcophagus and pursue the defiler wherever he or she went, eventually wreaking violence and murder on them for their crime.

Such stories had remained in localized Egyptian folklore for a number of centuries, but it suddenly and rather spectacularly shot to prominence in the Western mind in 1922. In this year Egyptologist and archaeologist Howard Carter finally discovered the tomb of Tutankhamen after a 15-year search. Although many of the tombs of the Pharaohs had been discovered and explored in previous centuries, Carter was still certain that the boy-king's tomb lay still undetected in the Valley of Kings; in 1907, backed by the wealth of

The Mummy

Lord Carnavon, he set out to find it, and in November 1922, he did so in some style. The opulence of the tomb was staggering and caused great excitement in the archaeological and Egyptology worlds. However, it was here that the alleged Curse of the Pharaohs came to haunt him. It was said that an inscription in hieroglyphics had been found in the tomb: "Death shall come on swift wings to him who disturbs the peace of the King." Thus, having broken into the site, Carter and his backers were at risk from some ancient retribution that stretched out of the aeons to destroy them. In actual fact, there had been no such warning, but there had been a number of local legends about Tutankhamen's tomb, and these fed into a popular mythology that seemed to grip the imagination of many people in the West. Egypt was still an ancient and mysterious land to many people and the idea of some ghastly curse, perhaps backed by the physical "presence" of some shrouded mummy, held an awful appeal. The curse seemed to gain some credence when Lord Carnarvon, who had financed Carter's expedition, suddenly and mysteriously died. Fanciful stories began to circulate: He had been somehow strangled by a guardian mummy and this face was deliberately being kept from the public; or some sort of ghastly figure had come out of the tomb and followed him halfway across the world.

In reality, Lord Carnarvon had been bitten by a mosquito while he was in Egypt—the wound had almost healed, but he accidentally cut it while shaving. Blood poisoning set in, leading to His Lordship's eventual demise. The curse seemed to strike again in 1924 when another financier—George Jay Gold—appeared to die in mysterious circumstances after visiting the tomb. There were also rumors that many of those who had been present at the opening of the tomb, including Carter himself, had met bizarre and untimely ends. In reality, only eight of the 58 people who had been present at the opening died shortly afterward, and all of those were from natural causes. Carter himself lived until 1939, when he died of lymphoma at the age of 64. Nevertheless, the idea of a curse, inextricably linked to the notion of a bandaged cadaver rising from its tomb, had become indelibly imprinted on popular imagination.

Hollywood's Interpretation

One of the more influential areas that was captivated by these stories was Hollywood. The Curse of the Pharaohs might have been suspect, but it was still a moneymaker for the film industry. With Carter's fabulous discovery still creating news and excitement many years after, the film companies turned their attention to the horror that allegedly rose out of the Egyptian desert. Even though there had been a number of lesser films dealing with the subject before, the first of the great "Mummy movies"—simply entitled *The Mummy*—appeared in 1932. It was directed by Karl Freund and starred the legendary Boris Karloff, long considered to be a "Master of Horror." This placed the image of the shambling corpse, bent on vengeance against unwitting Westerners, firmly within European culture. A number of other films were to follow—*The Mummy's Hand* (1940, starring B-movie cowboy hero Tom Tyler as the Mummy); *The Mummy's Tomb* (1942, starring the celebrated Lon Chaney, Jr., who would also star in subsequent mummy movies); *Mummy's Ghost* (1944), and *Mummy's Curse* (also 1944). Although not as popular as the vampire or werewolf, the mummy was still able to create terror and certainly established itself in horror culture of the era.

Recently, the idea of the mummy seems to have gained a fresh impetus with the release of Stephen Sommers's *The Mummy* (1999) and *The Mummy Returns* (2001). The films generated a mass of tie-in books and merchandise, much of which is still circulating. In the commercial world, it seems, the notion of the shambling corpse is still a lucrative one.

With the addition of the mummy, the perception of the walking cadaver was now almost complete, and the returning dead were now inextricably linked with evil and threat in the public perception. They further represented all that was alien and terrifying, and their appearance signaled no good for ordinary people. But there was one last—and important—element to add to the mix, an element that would, for many people, define the walking dead and what they were about. This element came out of Afro-Caribbean religion and folklore; it was the concept of the zombie.

3

Le Gran Zombi

Arguably, the most prevailing image of the walking dead is that of the zombie—the walking dead man of Haitian and African culture. Through the years, the zombie has been inextricably linked with voodoo, which is usually taken to be an African/Caribbean spirit religion with overtones of black magic. Similar to the mummies or the walking cadavers of medieval lore, the zombies are usually looked upon as being extremely violent and may even resort to cannibalistic practices at times. This is the impression that has come down to us through countless books and films, but is it actually true? Can such things truly exist? And is the zombie a physical manifestation of some old and

Walking Dead Man

dark religion, carrying out the orders of its mysterious priests? The answer is more complex than it might at first appear.

Although it is quite fashionable in most films and stories to portray voodoo (or hoodoo, as it is sometimes rendered in American fiction) as some sort of Pagan religion that worships evil gods and employs questionable rituals—some allegedly involving cannibalism and human sacrifice—the actual voodoo concept is rather different. Before considering the walking dead of African or Caribbean lore, something needs to be said about the voodoo idea as a whole.

Voodoo

Even though it is often portrayed as such, the concept of voodoo is not actually a religion at all. Rather it is an umbrella term for a number of spirit-based beliefs and interpretations that have emerged out of Africa and South America. These beliefs include candomle and umbanda (Brazil); arara (Cuba); shango (Cuba and Puerto Rico); and santeria, lukumi, and Mama Wata (the Caribbean and parts of West Africa). There is also a belief system known as voudoux or voudou, which is today the official religion of the West African country of Benin (formerly known as Dahomey and part of French West Africa until 1975). And although such perceptions certainly owe their origins to the tribal religions of the African peoples who traveled across the Caribbean as slaves, they have absorbed many traditions from Western Christianity as well. So although the central core of the religion may well lie in the African spirit world, much of the structure and ritual of the belief may run parallel to Catholic Christianity, which was, after all, the faith of the slaver owners and of those who brought the Africans to Latin America and the Caribbean as slaves.

And just to complicate matters even further, there are a number of different strands of voodoo belief, each influenced by the area in which it has grown up. We often associate voodoo beliefs with the Haitian Republic, a section of the island of Hispaniola in the Caribbean, which once boasted large slave plantations and which many consider to be its ancestral home, but there are other variants. For example, there is a slightly different belief system in New Orleans and in the bayou country of western Louisiana. Another variant comes from South Carolina, where the Gullah peoples from Angola worked as slaves on the plantations. And yet another variation is to be found in West Africa itself where it takes a number of forms.

Although the central feature of voodoo is that it is spirit-based (that is, spirit beings come and go through the world interacting with humans as they see fit), all of the aforementioned forms have drawn from a whole range of African and Creole influences. Thus, variants of Caribbean voodoo may contain the healing elements of the water spirits of Mama Wata, a belief found in parts of Burkina Faso (the former West African Republic of Upper Volta). Although New Orleans voodoo may contain some fortune-telling and precognosticatory elements of santaria and lukumi, found on many of the Caribbean islands and in South America. Many have been adapted to suit the perceptions, hopes, and aspirations of the situations in which the believers found themselves.

Furthermore, although it drew on the central tenets of the "pure" spirit religions from places such as Dahomey, Nigeria, and Angola, voodoo was in many respects a slave perspective. It was the "religion" of many of those who had been brought from Africa, mainly by European and Islamic slaves to work on the great plantations in Southern and South America as well as in the

Caribbean. These slaves picked cotton and gathered sugarcane and rice for mostly Christian employers who owned them outright, and who, in some cases, forced them to accept the Christian faith, which some did in a token capacity. However, their real belief was voodoo.

Given its fragmentary nature and the fact that it was mostly practiced by slaves, voodoo lacked the religious structure that characterized other faiths and belief-systems. It did not, for example, have official ministers or priests in the conventional sense—although there were unofficial "priests," both men and women, among its practitioners; it did not have regular, established, or recognizable meeting places, and its gatherings were often held in secret and in isolated places on the various plantations. This, of course, led to allegations among some people that the voodoo worshippers were engaging in some sort of Satanic practice such as summoning up devils or consorting with dark primal forces.

Voodoo was also considered to be a "political" belief. This was quite understandable. Many Caucasian planters lived in great and sprawling estates on which large numbers of slaves also dwelt. The balance between owner and slaves was often an uncertain one at best—the slaves might rise up (as they did in some parts of the Caribbean) and overthrow the owners, taking over the plantation for themselves. This was always a great fear amongst the Caucasian, slave-owning populace and anything that stirred the slaves up was to be discouraged. Voodoo was counted among these incendiary beliefs. Most plantation owners knew very little about it, but it was considered to be a heady mix of Pagan religion and African nationalism, perhaps fuelled by the consumption of raw alcohol, which was believed to form a part of its ritual. The so-called "voodoo priests" were whipping up their followers into some sort of murderous frenzy, and were urging them to turn on their owners. Such ideas only added to the belief that voodoo was somehow connected with evil and black magic, which was trying to subvert the truth and purity of Christianity. Stories circulated in major Christian churches that the Devil gave the followers of the belief supernatural powers through which they could do harm to their owners and create mayhem in God's ordered world by magical means.

The roots of the voodoo "religion" are believed to lie in the beliefs of the Ewe peoples, who inhabited an area that was known as Old Ghana many centuries ago (the areas of Mali and Mauritania and parts of Ghana today), although today their descendants inhabit areas of Ghana, Togo, and Benin. The origins of these people are extremely obscure, but they are thought to have migrated from Egypt somewhere around the 13th century. They settled around the Volta River and developed a culture that gave rise to the Fon, Ewe, and several other related tribes, all of whom share a common language-form. The word *voodoo* is thought to have derived from the Fon dialect and simply means "spirit," although several other French derivations and meanings have also been suggested.

The area was indeed occupied by several European colonial powers—England, France, and Portugal—and this influenced both the character and nature of culture that emerged there. The belief that has grown out of the word *voodoo* is a syncretic one, in that it attempts to make sense of the world around individuals by unifying the disparate elements of physical existence into a cohesive whole through the work of spirits. The spirits are everywhere, according to the voodoo tradition, and they intervene in the affairs of the mortal world on a regular basis. They are often capricious and prefer small children, and they are easily flattered or raised to anger. Some are benevolent

toward humans, others can be placated and flattered by humans, and some are implacably hostile towards humans. All of them, however, can shape human destiny, for good or bad, and all are susceptible to supplication by recognized practitioners and spirit summoners. In some cases they possess the physical bodies of those who had contact with them in order to achieve their purpose. It is the actions of these spirits (the "voodoo") that holds the universe together.

Lemba

Closely related to the basic voodoo beliefs of Western Africa are the central tenets of lemba, a belief-system that was mainly based on the Congo River in the central-west part of the continent. The river takes its name from the Kongo people who once inhabited the area (the name *Kongo* means "hunter") and who founded an ancient kingdom there. This formed what is today the Central African Republic of Congo and part of Angola, from which a distinctive culture emerged. Although Kongo beliefs also centred on the spirit world, it was subtly different to those of Old Ghana and western Africa. In the lemba perception, the central spirits are not wholly the forces of nature as they are in voodoo, but rather the spirits of dead ancestors. In strict lemba teaching only Nzambi Mpungu—the supreme high being—has always existed outside of time and space. All other spirits and supernatural forces have formerly existed in the world at some stage or other. In fact, some of the most powerful spirits (bakulu) are ancestors who died many centuries before. Similar to the spirits of voodoo, these ghosts or souls can be appealed to and can perform supernatural feats if the mood takes them. Throughout the years, this belief in the spirit ancestors became entwined with other ideas, such as a spirit of place or wandering air spirits.

When Nzinga Nkuwu, one of the kings of the Kongo, converted to Christianity in 1491, the belief-system underwent a major change. King Nzinga insisted that all his people practice the Christian faith, and so they did, adapting it so that they might continue with their old faiths and beliefs. The dead, in this syncretic faith, became akin to saints who could be called upon for favors and could actually, from time to time, take on a physical presence to enable them to intervene. It was thought that it could possess the living or take over objects in order to fulfil their wishes and will.

This, to some extent, was also a feature of voodoo belief, with which lemba was intermingled, and gradually the notions of the returning dead and the spirits who came and went through the world became fused together. Ideas of spirit possession were common in both traditions and the idea that the dead might be summoned, perhaps in a physical form, gradually became more widespread.

African Diaspora

As has already been noted, the voodoo belief system does not pertain to formal clergy such as ordained ministers or priests. Nevertheless, an informal clerical structure exists, consisting of those who have direct contact with the spirits and who know their moods and will. These are the successors of the local shamans in the homeland villages of Africa—those who had been able to converse directly with the spirits or who had been possessed by them. They are known as houngans, bokors (male), and mambos (female), and their powers are believed to be almost as potent as those of the spirits themselves.

Voodoo spread to America and through the Caribbean through what came to be known as the African Diaspora. From the late 17th century, through the 18th, and into the early 19th, there was a steady demand in these areas for slave laborers to work in the cotton, rice, and sugar cane plantations that were fuelling both the American and European economies. African slaves in particular fetched high prices, and so the coasts of the continent were systematically raided by slave-hunters who carried men and women away to work on the great estates of the New World. The slaves brought their own belief-systems with them, which flourished on the plantations, developing into unified voodoo cults that reflected the areas in which their plantations were situated—whether it was in the Caribbean islands, America, or Brazil. For example, many of the slaves in the American cotton plantations of Mississippi were of Ewe origin, whereas many of those working on the rice estates of South Carolina were of Kongo or Gola descendancy. Some of those who worked in the South American coffee plantations were of Yoruba origin, but, though the names of the spirits were different, their powers and influences were essentially the same.

Haitian Beliefs

One of the best-known forms of voodoo (or voudoun) is the Haitian strand that has its roots in the belief systems of Dahomey (Benin). This belief system has been made famous in the West through countless films and novels, and is supposedly the form that is closest to the ideal of curses, deadly charms, and zombies.

The Haitian Republic makes up part of the island of Hispaniola in the Caribbean, and, although now extremely poor, it was once the site of numerous wealthy sugar cane plantations. It was initially known as Ayiti (Land of Mountains), which is a name that was used by the indigenous Tiano peoples to describe their homeland. The island was discovered by Christopher Columbus on December 5, 1492, and was originally a Spanish protectorate. Indeed, one of the earliest colonists there was Columbus's brother Bartholomew, who founded a settlement based around a church dedicated to St. Dominic. However, large numbers of French buccaneers used Hispaniola as a base, establishing a large colony there and allowing France entitlement to part of the island.

In fact, at the same time they were condemning piracy the French government secretly dealt with a pirate chieftain named Guillaume Barre to establish large buccaneer enclaves on the western part of the island in defiance of Spanish rule. Frequent raids on Spanish shipping by French-backed pirates and the expansion of their enclaves meant that some sort of accommodation had to be reached, and this was done in 1697 in the Dutch town of Ryswick, as a treaty was signed granting a greater part of the island to the Spanish (the Dominican Republic) and the western third portion to the French (Haiti), which they called Saint-Dominogue.

Many of the pirate colonies now took to growing both tobacco and sugar cane, and the rise in the prices of these commodities, coupled with the easy availability of land in the west of Hispaniola, drew many French colonists. Between 1713 and 1787, more than 30,000 French colonists arrived, establishing themselves and turning Santo Domingo into one of the richest areas in the Caribbean. The island's tobacco and sugar industries boomed and great plantations grew, which produced crops for export.

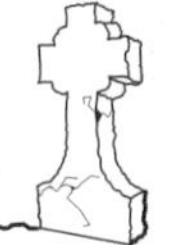

Plantations

Concomitant with this rising trade was a growth in slavery. Slaves were needed to work in the plantation field and gather in the crops, and soon Haiti was full of slave ships carrying human cargo, mostly taken from West Africa, which provided an almost infinite resource for the slaves. Thousands of black slaves arrived at the Haitian plantations, usually owned by French masters, and the black population steadily grew. In fact, in the eyes of the French colonists, it was growing to dangerous proportions, for the number of slaves on the island was now becoming higher than the number of French; fears of a slave rebellion mounted.

Haiti was not the only slave-holding region of the Caribbean. The British also maintained a number of island and American mainland plantations that depended heavily on slaves, and, similar to the French, they too feared revolt. In 1667, the British government passed a series of codes that were designed to regulate the behavior of slaves on their plantations. Shortly afterward, many other countries, including the French, adopted similar legislation. This meant that, if slaves attempted to run away, they could be brought back and severely disciplined. Although the result of this was certainly to keep the slave population in subjection on many plantations, it also drove the African culture underground, and made them dependant upon their own "religion" and spiritual (in the literal sense) leaders. This belief system borrowed from the Catholic faith of their French masters and it is possible to find elements of European culture within the main voodoo belief—sometimes in the language, and sometimes how the "religion" is structured. What emerges then is a heady mix of ancient Pagan gods from western Africa and French Catholicism.

Loa

The spirits in Haitian voodoo are known as *loa*, and they are a mixture of entities that have existed since the dawn of time (similar to gods) and the souls of dead ancestors. These loa come and go at will between the spirit world and our own; for the most part, they are invisible, but sometimes they take over the physical bodies of their followers for their own purposes. If there was a supreme being in this form of voodoo then it was Bondye (many have argued that this is a localized corruption of the French god *Bon Dieu*), who existed outside of time and space but who oversaw the loa in a kind of patriarchal sense. This entity was looked on in the same way that formal religions might look on God, Jehovah, or Allah. Some Haitian practitioners argue that Bondye does not really exist; this is simply part of the affect of the Christian French colonial culture on the native African traditions—and that the *real* supreme power is Damballa (or Damballah Weddo), who is the supreme loa. Damballa is also the spirit of fertility, of serpents and rainbows, and was probably originally a god or entity that was worshipped by the slaves who were brought from Dahomey. Damballa is sometimes portrayed as a great serpent, and is known in folklore as "Le Gran Zombi" or "Li Zombi." This *may* be the origin of the word *zombie*, which may not actually initially refer to the walking dead, but rather to an eternal spirit of resurrection and renewal that had the power over life and death.

Damballa's partner in the voodoo pantheon is Erzulie Freda, who is the patron of flowers, dancing, and music. She is also the spirit who is responsible for returning growth and, although Damballa is only one of her consorts (she has three) she exerts great influence over him. The beliefs of her followers are not far removed from those of some of the ancient fertility and

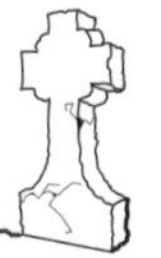

resurrection beliefs that flourished in early Middle Eastern times. Indeed, she may preside over the resurrection of the dead who reemerge from their graves, just as a plant dies and reemerges from the earth. There is, however, yet another element of Haitian voodoo that is tangentially concerned with resurrection from the dead.

Papa Legba

This is Papa Legba, the Lord of the Crossroads. In many respects, Legba is viewed as the intermediary between the world of the living and the world of the loa, particularly the spirits of the dead. He is the "Opener of the Way" between the two worlds and acts as a kind of gatekeeper for loa or spirits wishing to cross from one plane of existence into the other. Often portrayed as an old man leaning on a crutch or (in Benin and Nigeria) as a young and virile man with goats horns, he is one of the most potent symbols in Haitian voodoo. He connects the world of the living to Guinee, the Haitian Underworld from which the spirits or loa of the dead often rise up, seeking entry into the mortal world. Guinee (not to be confused with Guinen, the voodoo Paradise that lies underwater just off the Haitian coast) is the home of both the loa and the dead; it lies on the other side of the mirror, centered around the invisible city of life—Lavilokan—which conversely is the abode of the dead. Spirits of the dead return through mirrors or reflective surfaces to possess the bodies of the houngan, the bokor, or the mambo, and make their wishes known. Such interventions are usually accompanied by heavy drinking and loud drumming, which were also features of the African culture.

Lavilokan

Rada and Petra

And just to confuse things even further, two types of voodoo exist in Haiti. The first is based around the belief systems previously outlined and is known as Rada. The name is probably a corruption of Arada, a region in Dahomey from which many of the slaves were brought, and contained many of the beliefs of the Ewe, Fon, and related peoples. It concerns itself mainly with healing and exorcism and is, in many ways, considered to be a very positive aspect of the voodoo ideal. This strand of the belief relies heavily on the French traditions of the island, using many French words and concepts in order to explain its essential truths. The second branch is known as Petro or Petra voodoo, sometimes known as "Spanish voodoo." This is a darker and much more aggressive type of tradition, and there is an interesting folktale regarding its origins.

Although Haiti is essentially French, the island was originally Spanish, and many of the Spanish influences were retained. There were, for instance, a number of Spanish plantations that imported slaves to work in the cane fields. The legend states that, on one occasion, a slave known as Don Pedro drank large quantities of rum mixed with gunpowder (this was not an unusual mix for the famous pirate Captain Edward Teach—Blackbeard—who enjoyed a similar tipple) and began to dance wildly, summoning rather dark loa to him. Don Pedro later became a great bokor, dabbling in black magic, and his famous *Danse de Don Pedro* (which became the foundation for the Petro voodoo strand) was used to summon unwholesome spirits and the dead to do the bidding of the magician. Petro voodoo is sometimes known as Kongo voodoo, and this may suggest some aspects of the beliefs of different slaves from the Congo River. It is this Petro voodoo with which many Westerners are perhaps more familiar through grisly and lurid books and films. And although the Petro belief system in many ways parallels the Rada tradition, there are subtle variations and additional gods and loa. One figure (or figures) of note is (are) the *guide*, *Ghede*, or *Papa Ghede*. This is a confusing entity or series of entities (depending on what strand of the belief is followed), which has transferred to New Orleans voodoo and which forms a central tenet of the Petro tradition. In some accounts of the belief, the guede are a collection of loa who are strongly connected with the dead and who are charged (by either Damballa or Bondye) to escort the dead to Guinee. Although vague and unnamed in pure Haitian voodoo, they can nevertheless make their presence felt by possessing the bodies of the living or occupying the corpses of the dead—the essence of the zombie story.

In other traditions, Ghede or Papa Ghede is a single entity who functions very much in the same style as Papa Legba, and in fact the two are sometimes interchanged in the voodoo mind. Papa Ghede has the power over life and death, and is closely connected with the concept of resurrection and bringing the dead back from the grave. He is a dark and malevolent entity who can only be placated with copious amounts of rum and money. Ghede has a virulent hostility to all things European, and often is said to wait at the crossroads for passing white folk to whom he can do some mischief. He is also said to be the spirit of the first black man who ever died, and is usually portrayed as a short, stocky man in a tall hat, smoking a large cigar, and holding an apple in his left hand.

Petro voodoo is perhaps the most political of the two strands. In August 1791, Haiti erupted in a major slave revolt following the sacrifice of a black pig to the loa of Ezili Dantor—a goddess who was worshipped on some of the larger plantations. She is the Petro goddess of motherhood and is sometimes

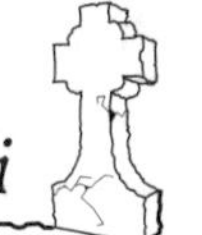

referred to as the "Creole Madonna." The sacrifice was carried out by the influential houngan, Dutty Boukman, who was later beheaded by the French authorities, but became one of the loa himself. Most of the violence that defined the risings was partly fueled by raw alcohol, which forms a central part of the Petro belief and was distilled from the sugar cane that was grown on the plantations themselves. This was one of the times when both strands of the island voodoo tradition had come together in a spontaneous act of violence and rebellion. The targets of their revolution, which would continue sporadically until 1803, were the plantation owners and the "petits blancs," or white men of lesser influence—shop owners, shipping agencies, and so on. There were many stories from this time, which were extremely spurious.

There were stories, for example, that local houngans had used the walking dead in order to overthrow troops sent against them, and that some of their followers had practiced cannibalism. All these tales were, of course, designed to create antipathy toward the Creoles and to generate a sense of alarm, so that more troops could be brought in to put down the rebellion. It did, however, link the practice of voodoo in the Caribbean with the idea of witchcraft and sorcery. The risings would continue until January 1, 1804, when the slave leader and commander Jean-Jacques Dessalines declared Haiti an independent republic. The loss of the colony, together with the reparations paid by the French and the new Haitian governments to plantation owners who had lost their property, was a severe blow to French interests in the Caribbean. Faced with such a catastrophe, the colonial authorities searched around for some sort of excuse for their failings. The slaves had, they suggested, appealed to ancient and barbarous gods.

Such beliefs fired up the slaves and inspired them to commit "terrible and heathenish atrocities" against good Christians. They had also used "dead men" or "zombies" in their rebel forces. Whether this referred to the actual walking dead or to some ordinary people whose senses had been taken away by arcane means is unclear, but these outlandish tales were actually believed back in France (and elsewhere) and were ascribed to "native magic," giving voodoo an even darker name. Although it is unlikely that either Dessalines (who became the new Haitian President) or a former slave leader, Toussaint L'Ouverture, were voodoo houngans, as has been suggested by some writers such as Michael S. Laguerre, or that they had the power to raise the dead, there is little doubt that, beneath the political surface, the power of voodoo still lingered on.

Politics

Indeed such power lay beneath the political surface until recent times, due to the rise to power of Francois "Papa Doc" Duvalier in 1957. Duvalier, who would rule Haiti dictatorially until 1971, was considered by many to be a great voodoo magician with a direct line to the loa and ruled his country by fear. Those who met with him in the presidential rooms in Port-au-Prince state that he kept a human skull on his desk as a symbol of his power and in order to cultivate that image. His secret police, through which he suppressed any dissent, were widely known as the Tonton Macoute, which ironically was a nickname representing something much more friendly. Tonton Macoute or Uncle Gunnysack in Caribbean folklore referred to a gift-bringer who came to young children—almost like a Haitian Santa Claus; later in the Duvalier era it became a standard nickname for a bogeyman.

The Macoute, correctly named the MVSN (Milice de Voluntaires de Securite Nationale) and under the command of Duvalier's longtime friend Luckner Carnbronne, were greatly feared and according to local lore, because their ranks contained some dead men whom Duvalier had personally raised from the grave. This idea, of course, added to the sinister reputation of the Macoute and to that of the Duvalier regime, serving to keep it in power. When Francois died in 1971, he was succeeded as ruler of Haiti by his son, Jean-Claude or "Baby Doc," who was allegedly not such a great a voodoo master; some time afterward the House of Duvalier collapsed in a popular revolt. In 1986, Baby Doc fled into exile in France and the Macoute faded away—some said that some of them had returned to their graves awaiting "Baby Doc's" return. This remains the case today with the House of Duvalier still in exile, unlikely to establish itself in Haiti again.

American Establishments

Many of the precepts of Haitian voodoo also established themselves in America—particularly around some of the coastal cities of Louisiana, which was a massive slave area. Many slaves also found their way to South Carolina to work on the rice plantations, and the city of Charleston also became something of a voodoo center. But it was cities such as New Orleans—a mysterious, colourful, and turbulent city even at the best of times—and the bayou country surrounding it where the voodoo flourished. And it was, in many respects, the more ferocious form of Petro voodoo that flourished there, concerning itself with curses and charms (gris-gris). There were also hints of cannibalism out in the swamps and bayous where voodoo cannibal cults such as *le cochon gris* (the grey pig—human flesh) were supposed to thrive. The inaccessibility of the swamps led an element of mystery to such beliefs. They provided a dark haven for slaves who had managed to escape from the ports or from some of the plantations, and it was thought that a Creole community, vastly opposed to white people, now lived deep in the bayou heartland, ready to strike against civilized society at any time. It was said that in hidden graveyards in the depths of the bayous, mambos, and houngans, and the descendants of runaway slaves raised cadavers to some form of life in order to do their evil bidding by calling on ancient African gods. This would later become the stuff of fiction and cinema, but in the 19th century it was considered a reality.

Le Baron

And in America, some relatively new loa were added to the voodoo pantheon. One of these was rather significant with regard to the dead. This was Baron Cimetiere, Lord of the Cemeteries, and, according to some accounts, master of the zombie. Le Baron, as he is known, is unquestionably an American voodoo adaptation of the Haitian Baron Samedi, who in turn was supposedly an adaptation of Papa Legba. He is also known in some parts of New Orleans as Baron La Croix.

In many respects, Baron Samedi (and by connection, his other incarnations) is the Haitian embodiment of death. The name Samedi is taken to mean "Saturday," although a number of other interpretations have also been offered. He is usually represented as a tall figure, in a European long black dress coat with a tall, black top hat, but with the face of a skull. Sometimes his face is shriveled and mummified, with the nose plugged, the mouth sewn shut, and wearing dark glasses (in other words, the face of a corpse prepared for burial Haitian-style). He carries a cigar in a long holder in one hand and a bottle of rum in the other, making him the epitome of European sophistication. He often loiters in the gateways of churchyards as if waiting for the arrival of the latest burial, which he then brings under his power unless the proper ceremonies are conducted by the dead person's family. This usually involves leaving

Baron Samedi

offerings of libations (mainly rum), cigars, and money in order to distract the powerful guede. In many Petro pantheons, Le Baron is married to Maman Brigitt or Le Gran Brigette, who is the embodiment of approaching death and who frequently takes the form of a black rooster. She collects souls on his behalf over which he then has great power. And should he choose, Baron Samedi has the power of resurrection, and can call cadavers from the grave at any time to enforce his will. Similar to many of the other guede, Le Baron communicates with his followers through a string of expletives and obscenities. When in power in Haiti, Francois Duvalier frequently adopted the appearance and persona of Baron Samedi, which served to increase the fear and awe with which he was viewed by the Haitian peoples.

Babalu Aye

Although Baron Cimetiere is usually portrayed as a sophisticated European, some older incarnations of him exist. One of these is Babalu Aye who often appears wearing more traditional native garb. Babalu is a loa from Yoruba and Fon traditions (although he also appears in Bantu folklore) who presides over fatal diseases, life, and death. He is one of the spirits who appears in Cuban Palo Mayombe, which is an *orisha* (spirit) religion that is found in Latin America and some Caribbean islands. He also appears in some Puerto Rican forms of Santaria, where is he is known as St. Lazarus, emphasizing his power over the dead and his partial connections to the Christian religion. Similar to Baron Cimetiere, Babalu can call the dead from their graves and bend them to his will.

Voodoo Practitioners

In New Orleans, voodoo was carried out by a number of recognized practitioners, all of whom claimed to have direct contact with the loa or the guide, and many of whom added their individual and idiosyncratic bits and pieces to the central core of belief.

Marie Laveau

The most famous of all these practitioners was the celebrated Marie Laveau, the self-styled *gran Mambo* and "witch queen of New Orleans." Marie Laveau is hard to date in the history of the city, because she may not have been a single woman at all, but *three* (or perhaps even *four*) different women (one of whom was her daughter) who took the established name (a bit like a voodoo trade name). Her dates are therefore given alternately as 1801–1881 and 1794–1897. It was, however, the figure of Marie who allegedly established the wild Petro form of voodoo in the city, attracting not only the New Orleans black community, but many respectable whites as well. In actual fact, all the Maries might be counted as brothel-keepers or "madams," and there was little doubt that prostitution went on at some of her gatherings in a house on Ann Street, but it was mixed with voodoo ritual and belief.

However, it was also said that one of the Maries, perhaps the first one—Marie Glapion Laveau (she had a common-law marriage to one Christophe Glapion)—conducted "special gatherings" out in the swamplands where black men and white women danced naked and interacted in some way with snakes. Indeed the first Marie was supposed to have kept a snake that slithered about her house, and which she called "Zombi." This, she claimed, was named after Damballah Wedo whom she referred to as "Le Gran Zombi"; the creature was supposed to be the embodiment of the loa. This *may* have been the first connection of the name to that of the walking dead, because Marie was supposed to have had the power to raise cadavers from their tombs. The gatherings at her house on Ann Street were usually very drunken affairs where copious amounts of rum (allegedly mixed with gunpowder, Petro style) were consumed.

Dr. John

Nor was Marie Laveau the only "voodoo queen" in New Orleans, for there were many other practitioners—both men and women—throughout the city. One of the most famous was Dr. John or Ol' John Bayou, from whom Marie was supposed to have inherited her powers. He was allegedly a severe, elderly "man of color," leaning on a cane with piercing eyes and formidable powers. He was a maker of gris-gris—parts of dead bodies ground to a *poudre* (powder) and tied up in a small muslin bag. This could either be a charm or a curse. It also had the power to raise the dead by drawing loa to occupy a cadaver at the behest of the voodoo magician. Consequently, Dr. John was also said to have the power of resurrection. Similar to Marie Laveau, Dr. John was said to have a great snake called a "zombie," which was supposedly the source of at least part of his powers.

He set himself up as babalawo (conjure man, the name being taken from the Yoruba word for "priest") and zombie master in a house on a plot of land that he had bought on Bayou Road. The place was full of animal and human skulls—the latter stolen from local graveyards—along with stuffed lizards and embalmed scorpions—all of which gave an air of mystery and menace to the man, and encouraged the zombie myth. Dr. John was important in the world of voodoo magic that the well-known writer Lafcadio Hearn, who may have been a lover of one of the Marie Laveaus, mentioned the passing of John Montenant (said to be Dr. John's real name). Hearne claimed extravagantly that Dr. John was more than 100 years old and that he had power to raise the dead (although he was probably around 81). The New Orleans R&B musician Malcolm Rebennac, who played in the early 1970s with Professor Longhair and his Shuffling Hungarians, later took the name Dr. John, which he still uses today. He claims to have been possessed by the loa of the Doctor to carry out his work in the world.

Joe Goodness

Dr. John, of course, had many rivals all across New Orleans, all claiming miraculous powers to match the doctor himself, and a number of them were just as colourful, such as Joe Goodness, Hoodoo Meg, Maman Calliba, Doctor Yah-Yah, and Zozo LeBrique. All of these people plied their voodoo trade in various parts of the city, claiming to cure ills and raise the dead. The intriguingly named Joe Goodness (the name was reputedly something of a

Voodoo Doll

misnomer, as there seems to have been little good about him) conducted secretive rites in the New Orleans of the 1850s. He claimed to be a zombie master and allegedly tore live chickens to pieces in order to be able to call forth cadavers from their graves. Dolls made from human skin—*puppe*—were supposedly used at some of the gatherings, and were reputedly imbued with a horrendous life, which gave greater impetus to the zombie legend.

John Domingo

Outside of New Orleans, another bustling voodoo city was Charleston, South Carolina. Here, the equivalent of Dr. John was John Domingo, or the Black Constable, who, in the late 1880s, presided over a reign of terror that ran far beyond the city itself. He had allegedly been a slave in the South Carolina Low Country, but had come to Charleston, where he had taken over a queerly shaped, shabby old house on Magazine Street on the corner of Mazyck Street (although it doesn't bear that name now). This place already had a questionable history, having formerly been a shop run by a Dutchman who had been forced back to Holland for some unmentionable crime. Some said that he, too, had been a black magician. Soon the Black Constable, as he styled himself, had become one of the foremost voodoo men in Charleston, allegedly more powerful than all his contemporaries, such as Dicky Breaux, Voodoo King of the Dorchester Road, or Cut Bread Jack, who lived on Charlotte Street.

Domingo was certainly an impressive-looking man, tall and powerfully built, and usually wrapped in a heavy Union greatcoat during the winter months. His hair was long and dirty with greasy strands that hung down onto his face. On the fourth finger of his right hand, he wore a large silver ring, carved in the

shape of a snake, which he referred to as "Le Gran Zombi," claiming that it had been forged in the Congo and that contained the power to raise the dead. It was said that in the old house on Mazyck Street (which was once extremely fashionable area, but, at the time Domingo dwelt there, became extremely run, down), Domingo performed terrible voodoo rites, which raised the dead and sent them out against his enemies. In fact several of those who spoke out against him came to rather suspicious ends.

His own end was extremely sudden and spectacular. In the late 1800s, he had become something akin to an unofficial lawman in the district (hence his nickname of the Black Constable) and people approached him to sort out their problems by magical means before going to the official law enforcement authorities. One evening he pursued two villains who were suspected of robbing a local resident. They tried to escape, but Domingo caught them and brought them back to Market Street, where a large crowd of onlookers had gathered.

"See,,,," he told them. "I am just like Jesus with a thief in either hand." He paused to consider something. "Only," he added, "I am much more powerful than Jesus." He seemed to want to say something else, but stopped and then straightened like a rod. A look of baffled bewilderment crossed his face and foam ran down from the corners of his mouth. Suddenly, he rose up on his toes as if something was dragging him upward; some bystanders swore that they saw the marks of long and inhuman fingers on his windpipe. The Black Constable gurgled before being thrown backward to the ground and before anybody could reach him he seemed to age and die; his face was said to have been the color of a withered cucumber.

He was carried into a local butcher shop and laid on the counter, where unsuccessful attempts were made to revive him; later a doctor was called and he was officially pronounced dead. As he lay there, his body seemed to shrivel and wither, becoming a fraction of its original size. It is therefore difficult to tell what became of the corpse, for by the time the police arrived it had gone. However, after those events nobody would buy meat from the butcher shop where his body had lain—they were afraid that it might be "touched" by John Domingo—and the butcher himself was later reduced to being a pauper with his business gone. No one knows where John Domingo is buried.

He was certainly far too wealthy from all his charms, poudres, and gris-gris, to be laid to rest in the paupers' field with the destitute of Charleston. Afterward, his eldest son hanged himself in a cowshed off Gadesden's Green, and his youngest son was poisoned in a house on Archdale Street. His ghost was often reported to be seen striding along Mazyck Street, the silver Congo ring flashing, but this was all probably just an old folktale told to frighten credulous people. Nevertheless, such tales left the area with a rather sinister spin, and with a connection to the walking dead. It was the dead, so the stories ran, who had killed John Domingo in retaliation for his abuse of their cadavers, and for his blasphemy. They had been invisible, but they had been physical nonetheless—how else would they have throttled the Black Constable?

Denmark Vassey

As in New Orleans, Charleston and the South Carolina Low Country boasted their fair share of voodoo practitioners, hoodoo queens, and conjure men, and danger always lay just below the surface of society. As in Haiti, voodoo and politics became linked. It was said that Denmark Vassey led the largest and most serious slave revolt in Charleston in the early 19th century. In the late 1700s, he won $1,500 in a charity lottery and used it to purchase his own freedom, setting himself up as a carpenter in Charleston. Inspired by the 1804

slave revolts in Haiti, which ended with the island being declared a republic, Vassey planned a similar rebellion in Charleston, which would free many of the slaves and overthrow the city authorities. In the panning of this revolt, he was reputedly aided by a voodoo houngan named Gullah Jack (*Gullah* being a contraction of the term *Angola*, denoting his African origins) who was supposed to have promised him an army of the dead to supplement his numbers. The revolt was due to take place on July 4, 1822 (which is Bastille Day in France), but details of the plans were leaked by two slaves who disagreed with Vassey's motives, and the authorities arrested 131 people in total.

In the end 67 persons were convicted and 35 hanged, including Denmark Vassey and Gullah Jack. However, there were whispers that the latter was not actually dead, but was ready to rise again from the grave, bringing an army of the Undead with him. Indeed, during the late 1920s and part of the 1930s a voodoo man practiced in Charleston under the name of Gullah Jack Pritchard, claiming to have been possessed of the loa of the original Gullah Jack, and also claiming to be able to raise the dead. He sprang to prominence during a trial for extortion, after which he was sent to jail—his trial, however, drew a fair amount of press attention and speculation due to his alleged "possession" and some of his claims regarding the dead.

Voodoo Doctors

In the Low County beyond Charleston, voodoo and the dead intermingled as well. Here the various "hoodoo doctors" allegedly knew rituals that would make the corpses buried in the isolated cemeteries of the region return to some form of hideous life. Places such as Beaufort County thrived with all sorts of conjure men: Dr. Bug, Dr. Antoine, Miss Delphine Paysandu, and the intriguingly named Old Mother Go-Go, who also sometimes operated on Trapman Street in Charleston. She is an interesting personality, because her followers (those who attended her gatherings) claimed that she had died some 50 years before, but had risen from the grave to become a voodoo queen. This made her, in effect, one of the walking dead, and greatly enhanced her voodoo reputation amongst those who visited her.

Dr. Buzzard and J.E. McTeer

The greatest of all the South Carolina voodoo doctors was unquestionably Stephaney Robinson, who died in 1947, and was known far and wide throughout the Low Country as Dr. Buzzard. He was famous for his ongoing magical feud with the sheriff of Beaufort County and the Low Country, J.E. (Ed) McTeer, Dr. Buzzard was a dapper little man of African descent who looked more like a minister in the African Methodist Episcopal (A.M.E.) Church than a voodoo houngan or "root worker." He was quite a wealthy man, and in 1943 he was described as an elderly, dignified gentleman "always dressed in quality black." McTeer, by contrast, had come (on his mother's side) from a South Carolina slave-holding family, the Heywards, and his forebears had signed the Declaration of Independence.

As a boy, he had witnessed the activities of the conjure-men and zombie-masters on his maternal grandfather's plantation, and was convinced of their powers. He was also convinced that he had certain powers that were more than a match for the supernatural ways of any houngan, including Dr. Buzzard. The battle between McTeer and Dr. Buzzard became the stuff of South Carolina legend, with one gaining the upper hand and then vice versa, but, in the end, fortune favored the Sheriff. After McTeer had donned blue sunglasses (blue being a prominent voodoo color) Dr. Buzzard's eldest son, who was famous

for his hedonistic lifestyle, drove his car across a causeway in a blinding rainstorm and drowned in a saltwater creek. Dr. Buzzard believed that the sheriff had cursed his family and strove to make peace.

Both Dr. Buzzard and McTeer were thought by many of those around them to have the powers of a zombie-master and could raise the Low Country dead when they chose; there seems little doubt that McTeer himself believed that, too. Stories about his miraculous powers continued to circulate after he had stepped down as sheriff, perhaps mainly to help sales of his memoirs, *Fifty Years as a Low Country Witch Doctor*, which he published after Dr. Buzzard had died. The preponderance of voodoo practitioners in several of the southern cities and sorcerous feuds such as McTeer and Dr. Buzzard, which was later rather widely and popularly publicized certainly brought home the concept of the walking dead, motivated by African magic, to the North American mind.

Voodoo Today

In America today, however, voodoo has become slightly kitsch. Voodoo shops in New Orleans and Charleston flourish, all claiming to sell the "secrets of the ages." Here such things as charms, amulets, and zombie memorabilia can be bought. Such items can be bought online as well—including such items as "goofer dust," which allegedly has the power to raise the dead. This ties in well with the idea of the zombie as a representation of the walking dead.

In the Caribbean, too, variants of voodoo continued to thrive even to the present day, but here the idea is taken more seriously. Here is it known as *obeah* or *obi*. Although often classed as two separate belief systems, voodoo and obeah are nevertheless very close. Indeed in some instances there appears to be little difference between obeah, Kongo, or Petro voodoo, and the practitioners of Petro are sometimes known as "obeah men." The name *obeah* is an Ashanti word meaning "sorcery" or "dark working," coming from rural Ghana. Obeah is to be found on various islands scattered across the Caribbean including the Virgin Islands, Trinidad and Tobago, and the Bahamas, and in countries such as Belize. Along with the curses and charms that were prepared, there was the alleged power to raise the dead; after doing so, they forced them to act as servants for the houngan, bokor, or obeah man, which was also a feature of Petro voodoo.

Le Zombi

It has been necessary to give this admittedly brief history of such a complex belief system in order to set the idea of the zombie—the walking dead man, which is our usual perception of such a being—in context. In its purest voodoo form "le Zombi" does not refer to the walking dead at all, but to a snake that is the embodiment of Damballah Wedo. Although there are tales in Haitian, American, and West Indian voodoo folklore concerning the walking dead, how were they enticed to rise from the grave? And what were they? Were they truly the cadavers of the dead person who had been buried, or were they motivated by some unholy *loa* or *ghede?* Were they, in effect, akin to the walking *corpus* of medieval Europe, motivated by some vindictive or malevolent spirit drawn by sorcery from the spirit world of Guinee? These were questions that have taxed (and continue to tax) the European mind.

The man who unquestionably brought notions of the Afro-Caribbean belief systems to the West, however, was William Buehler Seabrook (1884–1945). Seabrook was an extremely colorful and widely traveled individual who had worked at a number of jobs before beginning to write on the esoteric and the occult.

Born in Westminster, Maryland, he began his career in newspapers working as reporter and city editor on the *Augusta Chronicle* in Georgia. In 1915 he enlisted in the French army, but was discharged out after being gassed at Verdun in 1916. Nevertheless, he awarded the Croix de Guerre for his service. Returning to journalism, he became a travel writer, contributing articles to such publications as *Reader's Digest* and *Vanity Fair.*

As part of an assignment he traveled to French West Africa where he lived among a tribe called the Guerre, whom he claimed were cannibals. It was here that Seabrook claimed to have had his first taste of human flesh, for which he professed to have a liking. Whether this is true or not is open to question, but it gave him something of an exotic status among the travel writers of his day. By now, Seabrook considered himself to be a writer in the style of what Ernest Hemingway called "the Lost Generation": young writers and poets who had served in the First World War and who had gravitated toward Paris as a city of culture. He was also exhibiting a taste for the arcane, and, in 1920, he spent a week with Aleister Crowley, the celebrated English Satanist, occultist, and drug addict, which only seemed to inspire and excite him further. He was allegedly drinking heavily and using a lot of drugs, which seemed only to drive his passion further toward the occult.

He began to travel again, seeking out esoteric places and writing books and articles about them. In 1924, for instance, he traveled to the Arabian Peninsula where he lived among the Bedouin and the Yezidi, who had a reputation of being devil worshippers (worshipping Melek Tau, the Peacock Angel whom Christians have equated with Lucifer), an aspect that Seabrook certainly dwelled upon. The resultant book, *Adventures in Arabia: Among the Bedouins, Druses, Whirling Dervishes, and Yezidee Devil Worshippers*, was published in 1927, and, in keeping with much of his work, was a rather sensationalist mix of fantastic claims and hints at arcane knowledge and terrible rites.

Inspired by tales of Caribbean voodoo, he subsequently traveled to Haiti and in 1929 published a book on the subject that many count as a seminal work on the subject: *The Magic Island*. In this, Seabrook drew attention to a strange and sinister dark organization that he called Culte des Mortes (Cult of the Dead). This, he claimed, had originated in the earlier ancestor worship of Africa and was centered on spirit possession and the raising of the dead. Arguably, it was Seabrook more than anyone else who painted lurid pictures of wild and ecstatic dancing, mysterious incantations, and the dead rising and walking among the living.

Taking the Niger-Congo word *nzambi*, meaning "god" (which is probably the root of Le Gran Zombi as applied to Damballah Wedo) he used it to describe the risen cadaver, giving us our word *zombie*. The nzambi was, in all probability, a fertility god, linked to the changing of the seasons and to growth and may well have been associated with rebirth and resurrection. This probably fit in with the idea of returning from the grave and of risen corpses. Whether the Culte des Mortes actually existed or whether it existed in the way

that Seabrook said that it did is a matter that is open to question, but now the idea of a zombie as a walking dead person, strongly connected with voodoo practices, was beginning to germinate in the popular mind.

A section of the book entitled "Dead Men Working in the Cane Fields" was reprinted in several American magazines and journals portraying risen corpses working tirelessly in the Haitian cane fields at the behest of some bokor or zombie master and for no pay. It reinforced the image of the lumbering dead man—the image that we now traditionally associate with the zombie—without reason or thought, slavishly following the instructions of some Haitian sorcerer, and it filled the Western mind with dread—so much so that, inevitably, Seabrook's article and book formed the basis for the 1932 horror film *White Zombie*, which even today is regarded as the finest of the early film genre and has become something of a cult classic.

Was Seabrook's vision of the Haitian cane field workers true? Were there indeed corpses working there as unpaid labor? Perhaps part of the image went back psychologically to the old days when slaves worked, almost thoughtlessly, on the plantations in the West Indies. And of course, there is much speculation about the use of drugs. Could it be that the workers were not dead at all, but instead were "zombified" by using from some drug (known only to the voodoo bokors), which renders the victim extremely liable to suggestion and could give the appearance of death?

Perhaps as a result of his expeditions and writings (and possibly his own imaginings), Seabrook descended further into alcoholism and sadistic sexual practices. In 1933, he was committed at his own request to Bloomingdale, a mental sanatorium in Westchester County in New York State in order to seek treatment for his alcoholism. However, he discharged himself and wrote another book, *Asylum*, about the experience and treated it as if it were yet another foreign expedition. In 1935 he married Marjorie Ward Worthington, but the couple divorced in 1941 due to Seabrook's persistent drinking and his sadistic sexual demands. In 1945, William Seabrook committed suicide by overdosing on drugs while living in Rhinebeck, New York. But he had left a legacy behind him: the cultural legacy of the zombie.

Zombie Culture

Following Seabrook's death, a number of books and films all centered around voodoo, and zombies began to appear. *White Zombie* was the first of these, but it was not to be the last. Throughout the 1930s and 1940s, a number of films emphasizing the power of voodoo and the walking dead were released with such sensationalist titles as *King of the Zombies, Revolt of the Zombies*, and *Revenge of the Zombies*, culminating in 1943 in Jacques Tourneur's early zombie classic *I Walked with a Zombie*. Many of the plots were set in Haiti or other Caribbean countries, and involved white planters being killed and brought back to life through the power of voodoo, functioning as a kind a robotic figure that shambled along, carrying out the wishes of some malignant sorcerer. This was accompanied by books that played up the zombie theme and that, in most instances, followed the direction of the films and also of Seabrook's rather fantastic writing on the subject. Many also portrayed the zombies as being flesh-eating monsters, dwelling perhaps on the ideas of cannibalism, which had come out of Africa at the time. Books and stories with lurid titles such as *The Killing Dead, Where Zombies Walk*, and *Island of Zombies* appeared with sensationalist regularity throughout the late 1930s and 1940s, all following roughly the same pattern in content and plot. Most had the air of Gothic romances where heroes and heroines investigated

some decaying plantation house on some remote Caribbean island or the steamy swamps of the southern United States, only to find themselves trapped by the shambling dead.

New aspects of zombie lore were sometimes introduced—one of these being the zuvembie, which appeared in 1938 in a short story, "Pigeons from Hell" by noted fantasy writer (and creator of Conan the Barbarian) Robert E. Howard. This, according to the tale, was a kind of female zombie—somewhere between the walking dead and a witch—that lived in a crumbling southern mansion somewhere in the swamps. There *may* be such a creature in some voodoo folklore, but if there is, it is extremely obscure.

There were, of course, some serious and ethnographical works on the subject such, as the 1958 book *Voodoo in Haiti*, written by the French anthropologist Alfred Metraux. Metraux was a close friend of the notorious French "philosopher of evil," Georges Bataille—the infamous "Lord Auch" (literally, Lord to the Shithouse) and like Seabrook, he committed suicide in 1963. However, none of them really dealt with the matter of zombies. The lurid tales concerning the rising and wandering dead continued and took a hold on the popular imagination, particularly in the West.

One of the earliest films of recent times to develop and expand upon the zombie theme was *Night of the Living Dead*, released in 1968 and directed by George A. Romero—a director who was to make his mark with zombie/walking dead films. The plot is relatively straightforward—the brains of the recent dead are reactivated by some form of unspecified virus and the cadavers are brought back into a type of horrid life. A number of teenagers are trapped in a remote and abandoned farmhouse by a group of these mobile corpses who are hungry for their flesh. The film created something of a sensation when it first came out (it has gone on to become a cult horror classic) and established Romero's name as a horror director. The film was hailed as a "new dawn in horror" and spawned a host of substandard imitators, many of which were simply gorefests with names such as *Zombie Holocaust, Zombie Dawn Blood for the Zombie, The Hunger,* and *Flesh Eaters from the Tomb.* Thankfully most of them have not survived to the present time.

Romero would return to the subject of zombies and to the horror that they evoked 10 years later in his much-lauded *Dawn of the Dead* (1978), which was refilmed for release in 2004 by Zack Snyder. Although the remake had mixed critical reviews, it was a commercial success and remains one of the top-grossing American horror films. Once again, some form of unexplained virus reanimated the brains and bodies of the recently dead and caused them to turn on the living, devouring their flesh. Cities and centers of high population became death traps with a handful of survivors trapped in a shopping mall, reinforcing the immediate horror of the shambling dead in the minds of the viewers.

Spurred on by the lucrative franchise, Romero made another zombie film in 1985—a sequel entitled *Day of the Dead,* in which a number of scientific military personnel become trapped in an underground bunker by marauding zombies. The lukewarm critical reception that the film received deterred the director from making any further films until 2005, when he returned to the screen with *Land of the Dead.* This concerned a community in a post-Apocalyptic world who were surrounded by zombies—the walking dead, reanimated by some unknown disease—who were trying to break in. The film was a success and has inspired *Diary of the Dead,* which Romero released in February

Zuvembie

2008. This concerns a video diary released by a group of independent film-makers who are trapped by mindless zombies.

Romero is not the only successful film maker concerned with what might be described as "the zombie menace." In 2007, Damon Lemay's *Zombie Town* achieved some acclaim when he portrayed a town of dead people, resurrected and motivated by mysterious parasites. But the most notable contemporary film on the subject must be Francis Lawrence's *I am Legend* (2007). Based on the 1954 novel of the same title by Richard Matheson (and previously in 1971, *The Omega Man* directed by Boris Sagal), the film tells the story of Robert Neville, who believes that he is one of the few survivors of a fearsome plague that has mutated out of a cure for cancer in 2009. This has killed almost 90 percent of the world's population, only to resurrect them as flesh-eating zombies who can only travel at night or in the shadows. The film became a box-office success and further established the reputation the lead actor Will Smith as Neville.

A much more interesting and thoughtful film, however, is the 2004 French film *Les Revenants,* directed by Robin Campillo. In this, the dead rise from their graves in a small French town, but, instead of attacking the living, they attempt to reintegrate themselves into the society and into their former lives. It provides a completely new slant on the traditional zombie theme.

Concomitant with the zombie film revival was a rise in the interest of the walking dead through books and comics. A number of collections of zombie-centered mass-market paperbacks appeared with titles such as *Zombie Island, Terror of the Zombies,* and *The Restless Dead,* as well as a number of anthologies, all of which included Seabrook's "Dead Men Working in the Cane Fields." Some of these texts combined both scientific and voodoo themes, and introduced relatively new elements into zombie lore. For example, it was said that using salt might defeat zombies. There is no real evidence from

Haitian folklore that salt can affect the walking dead, although salt was often used in European lore as a protection against witchcraft and demon possession, and it *may* appear in some voodoo rituals, but this is not certain.

And there were specific zombie comics as well. One of the most notable (and finest) was *Deadworld,* which was released in the United States by Arrow Comics (and later by Caliber) during 1986–1987. It ran for at least six distributed issues. It featured a series of short zombie stories written by Gary Reed and brilliantly drawn by Vince Locke. Currently, a comic named *The Walking Dead,* published by Image Comics and written by Robert Kirkman and drawn by Tony Moore is enjoying much success. This features the community of Cynthiana, Kentucky, which is surrounded by a world in which zombies rule. The comic serves to establish the terror of the walking dead in both the popular mind and in popular culture once more.

Zombie Law

Just to confuse matters a little further, there was a common assumption that Haitian law had formally forbid the use of zombies as slave labor, and there was a statute to that effect. This led to the common belief that there actually *were* such creatures, that they were animated corpses, and that they might be used at the behest of someone using black magic. It served to strengthen the belief in the Haitian walking cadavers. In fact, Article 246 of the 1835 Haitian Penal Code (Codigo Penal de Haiti) reads as follows:

> *It shall be qualified as attempted murder the employment which may be made against any person of substances which, without causing death, produce a lethargic coma or less prolonged. If after administering such substances, the person has been buried, the act shall be considered as murder no matter what result follows.*

Although this law is generally and vaguely mentioned by some in order to support the existence of zombies in Haiti, it does not appear to relate to those who have actually *died*, but rather to those who have been *drugged* to such an extent that their vital functions have slowed down and they might be considered to be dead. Indeed, some may have been buried only to be "resurrected" later. Following this "resurrection" it is possible that some of those affected may have suffered brain damage from the effects of the drug.

In 1980, a Haitian man, Clairvius Narcisse, who had been dead and buried for 18 years, wandered into a village on the other side of the island from the place where he had been born, seemingly alive. He was recognized by his sister Angelina, who happened to live there, but, in a vague and disaffected state, he failed to recognize her. He had been wandering about Haiti for some time (some accounts state for as long as 16 years). According to the story, he had been given some form of *poudre* (psychotropic drug) in 1962 by his brothers—one of whom was a prominent voodoo bokor—following a dispute over some land. Two days later he was pronounced dead by two qualified doctors and was identified by his sisters Angelina and Marie-Clare; he was then buried in his home village of L'Estre.

Shortly after he was allegedly "resurrected" as a zombie. Directly after his "resurrection," Clairvius was sold to another bokor, who allegedly maintained an army of zombie slaves to work on his sugar plantation. However, as the effects of the drug started to wear off, he became more aware of his surroundings and was able to make an escape. However, he had not completely recovered his senses—he would, in fact, never do so—and spent much of his time wandering across the island in a confused state before stumbling into his sister's village.

Clairvius was examined by some local doctors, who suggested that he had received large amounts of some form of neurotoxin that had kept him in an almost paralyzed and highly suggestible state, which, at time, looked like death. His story was a rather incoherent one: He had been "raised from the grave" by his brother and sold onto the bokor who had regularly given him some "magical potion" in his food. When the bokor had died, Clairvius had regained a partial control of his senses and had made his escape. There seemed to be little doubt that he had been given some form of voodoo *poudre*, which had produced these effects and had apparently turned him into one of the "walking dead." Just what he had been given became a matter of great speculation.

Zombie Poisons

In the 1960s, it was assumed that "zombification" could be brought about by using the skin and internal organs of the puffer fish—considered to be the second most deadly creature on earth. Certain organs of the fish (also known as fugu in Japan and Asia) were deemed to secrete a toxin that could cause paralysis and death in humans; this was believed to be the main constituent of the zombie *poudre*, also known as "resurrection powder." However, in the 1980s and 1990s such a hypothesis was changed, and it was assumed that he had been poisoned with datura stramonium or jimson weed, a plant of the nightshade family, also known as the zombie cucumber. The plant generates scopolamine, a tropane alkaloid drug that is sometimes used in African medicines, but can also have disastrous, if not fatal, side effects. Concoctions incorporating small amounts of this substance are to be found in a number of rituals in West African folk tradition, which are said to induce death-like trances in which visions may occur. If ingested in large quantities it was suggested that it produced a paralysis that could be mistaken for death. The effects of datura have sometimes been described as "a living dream" in which the subject is awake, but is totally unconnected to the immediate world—an attitude that suggests the popular image of the zombie.

In the early 1980s, this led to the first "serious" book into zombie poisons, based around the then celebrated case of Clairvius Narcisse. This was *The Serpent and the Rainbow* published in 1985 by Canadian ethnographer Wade Davis. It would be made into a rather sensationalist, but critically acclaimed film in 1988, directed by the celebrated Wes Craven. The book was an attempt to discover some sort of "medicine" that might produce the walking dead of Haiti. Davies had surmised that Clairvius Narcisse had been "zombified" and turned into a "walking dead man" through the administration of datura. He had also assumed that there was an antidote to the effects of the toxin that could be produced by a derivative of the Calabar bean. (This turned out to be inaccurate.)

Although Davis's work contained merit in that it served to set the idea of the walking Haitian dead within some form of rational context, the work was ruined by his sensationalistic and rather overblown self-indulgent style. He tried to portray himself as a latter-day Indiana Jones—flying aircraft, and dealing with cannibals and headhunters in an attempt to find "secret mysteries," which had been previously denied to white men. In many respects, the book reads similar to an adventure tale, which is why it proved so attractive to filmmakers. And some of Davis's methods and evidence have been subsequently called into question by other academics. His work goes a little way to examining the zombie phenomenon, but, in the end, the creature still remains largely a mystery.

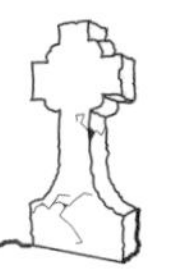

Do the Zombies Really Exist?

So, does the zombie actually exist? Is it truly the body of a dead individual, resurrected through some supernatural (or other) means? Despite the assertions of Wade Davis and others, many in the West still appear to think so. Certainly there have been many mysterious stories concerning the "walking dead" that have emerged out of Haiti and the Caribbean, and these have fed into the popular horror culture of writers and moviemakers. However, some of the "scientific mood" seems to have modified at least some of the plotlines. Where previously the zombies had been created by voodoo magic, other reasons are now being found for their existence, and as speculation with regard to germ warfare and biogenic weapons increases, the main origin for the "walking dead" now tends to be some form of unknown disease. The idea of some form of viral plague, killing people and then making them rise as zombies, is more in tune with the scientific mind of the late 20th century and has taken a firm grip on the popular imagination, pushing the bokors, mambos, and other practitioners of voodoo a little further into the background. Even so, the image of the zombie victim has remained pretty much the same: the vacant stare, the shambling gait, perhaps even with a taste for living human flesh. This is indeed the vision of the walking dead from zombie lore.

The idea of the zombie, then, carries on the terrifying tradition of the walking dead. It has reinforced the idea of the violent and malignant shambling form that appears in some other cultures—in the image, for example, of the Scandinavian draugr. The walking dead are, in many respects, viewed as hostile, malignant, and susceptible to those who would use them for evil purposes. This has been one of the supposed central tenets of voodoo. But is this perception universally held? Are there cultures in which a slightly different perspective might be held? It is to this question that we now turn.

4

The Living Dead

It has been already noted that, for many ancient peoples, physical death was not always perceived as the absolute end. In some cases, it was merely viewed as a transitionary phase, for, when life ceased on this moral level, it continued elsewhere, sometimes much as it had in this world, nor was it always the end of their involvement in the affairs of the living. Indeed, in some cases, the dead could actually *observe* what was going on from their vantage point beyond death and decide to take action in order to bring about a desired outcome. And of course, they could also be contacted by the living through priests and shamans, and called on for help or support.

The psychological impetus behind such beliefs is, of course, perfectly understandable. Many of us have those we value greatly and to whom we may look for assistance and support. Similarly there are those within the community to whom we might look and count on to "get things done," and upon whom we (and the community) become dependent. If such an individual is removed—say through death—we may feel a sense of loss or helplessness. Also if the individual concerned had a particularly strong personality or was something of a "character," then his or her loss is felt even more.

Individuals and/or communities might deal with this sense of loss in several ways. They may seek to "bring the individual back" through what might be described as "a sense of being"—the *spiritus* of medieval thinking. For example, some people may walk into a room or visit a spot strongly associated with a dead person and still feel his or her presence there. They may see nothing, but still have a sense of the person who is now dead. This feeling, in fact, forms the basis of many ghost stories. However, while *feeling* the presence of the departed was all very well, many people also wished to actually *see* a physical representation of the individual concerned. Therefore, some claimed to be able to view the *spiritus* of the dead as it passed through the world. Yet, for some, this was still not enough. They wished to see their ancestors in a *corporeal* state—the *corpus* of medieval lore—whether that be through possession of a living person or as a cadaver actually rising from its grave. This gave communities a reassurance that their protectors and sages had not forgotten about them and might still be physically involved in their affairs, just as they had been when alive.

In fact, some ancient cultures may very well have put the cadavers of their prominent deceased—their great heroes or wise people—on display for easy access and interaction. It has, for instance, been suggested that this was a facet of the Neolithic Bronze Age Windmill Hill culture in Wiltshire, England. Although not archeologically proven, there is a tradition that the dwellers in the hill forts of the area placed their dead in great earthen mounds, built around wooden structures where the dead could either sit or lie while "keeping an eye" on the settlement. While excavating the area in the 1920s (the site had been identified as Neolithic more than 60 years before), archaeologists found traces of an enclosure that may have been accessed by a type of causeway in which bodies might have been housed. This would keep the dead close at hand and perhaps invest them with some form of "communal life" along with their descendants. They could be consulted and, perhaps in times of community crisis—such as an attack—it was believed that they could rise up and defend the settlement. Archaeologists such as Mr. and Mrs. B.H. Cunnington, excavating in the areas later in the 1920s, had found similar enclosures on nearby Knapp Hill, which might suggest that the belief in the nearness of ancestors was quite widespread in the region. Perhaps these early people also believed that their admired ancestors could imbue the living with some of their inherent powers and attributes.

Celtic Beliefs

The ancient Celts certainly believed in this. For them, the dead were not all that far away, and great men (and women) always kept a protective eye over their people, standing ready to help if need be. This they did by projecting some of their attributes into those who came to consult them. This was usually done through what was known as a "head well."

For the Celts, the essence of a person lay not in his or her heart (as was later assumed—today we sometimes speak of someone "having a great heart")

Celtic Head of the Dead

but in the head. Consequently, the elements that made a person great, mighty, or wise lay in the head. But could such attributes—or indeed some of the personality of the individual—be passed on in some way? If they could the dead might gain some new form of partial life albeit in another body. Thus the head of the great person was placed at a well where people came to drink or to take home water, in the hope that the personality might be transferred into the community or to a specific individual who drank there, and thus the deceased might gain life once more. His or her strength or wisdom might be passed on from generation to generation in this manner. As the water poured over or swirled around the head or the skull of the dead, his or her personality waited for someone to come along and drink, so that it might enjoy life once more.

Crossroads

The gathering of the dead also occurs at crossroads. Of course, the idea of crossroads being linked with the supernatural and with supernatural entities is not exclusive to Polish or East European folklore. Many cultures—particularly Celtic culture—feature the crossroads in their mythologies as a place where fairies, ghosts, and the corporeal dead gather, sometimes to do harm to travelers and to passersby. Perhaps it is the symbol of the crossed roads that gives them this rather sinister and questionable reputation—one road leading to the world of the living and one road leading to the Afterlife. Indeed, in some folktales, crossroads form the boundary between this world and the one which is to follow. In places such as England, Brittany, Ireland, Wales, and Scotland, they are places to be avoided after dark for fear of encountering the dead.

As has been already noted Celtic lore is also full of tales of the corporeal dead. In Ireland, these were the *marbh bheo*—the night-walking dead. In many cases, these revenants were harmless and simply traveled the roads in a rather aimless fashion. Some did, however, return to their former homes, usually after their families had gone to sleep.

Ancestor Worship

This was the case of many other ancestors who watched from the Afterlife, seeking out some way that they might return to and interact in the world of the living. And the living were often aware of the interest in their affairs by the denizens of the world of the dead. Indeed sometimes they welcomed it and paid homage to those that had gone before them. This was known as "ancestor worship"—venerating ancestors in the hope that they might return or that they might perform some physical and beneficial task in the mortal world.

Today, ancestor worship is not universal, even among the less well-developed societies. The anthropological thinking of the later 19th century—Edward B. Tylor, Herbert Spencer, and Frank Jevons—deemed such beliefs as "primitive" methods of dealing with the unseen and honoring cultural traditions that were passed down through the generations. But deep beneath the scientific explanations, the fear of the dead still remained—a facet that anthropologists now acknowledge. Ancient ancestor worship was an ambivalent belief. We have already noted how ancient peoples looked to the dead for guidance and protection—however, they also feared the return of the dead. The dead might destroy, murder, or spread disease if they had a mind to, and in many such

cultures they were extremely unpredictable. At least part of the function of ancestor worship, therefore, concerned the placating of the dead and preventing them from doing harm to the living. This might take the form of festivals in which the returned dead could take part; this participation was usually believed to be in corporal form. Sometimes it was through spirit possession, and sometimes the actual cadavers themselves were supposed to interact with the living.

In a number of instances throughout Christian lands, such a return of the dead was also sanctioned by the Church, which had found itself caught in a rather awkward position: Although it disapproved of the Pagan elements of such worship, to deny it was also to deny the possibility of the Afterlife. It was better, therefore, to announce a feast day or festival on which the dead might return, which the church could control to some extent. These feasts and festivals also underscored the belief in immortality of the spirit, which was essential to the Christian message; this was similarly incorporated into the beliefs of a number of other religions, such as Islam, though not perhaps to the same extent.

Dead Festivals

Such a festival of participation between the living and the dead may well have been the origins of the celebrated Day of the Dead—El Dia de los Muertos—which takes place in Mexico on the first days of November (the old European festival of Halloween). Although it is said to be a Christian festival, based around All Soul's Night and All Saints Day (October 31st and November

Ist, and often extending into November 2nd); its roots may be more Pagan and may stretch back into Mesoamerican times. Some anthropologists have argued that it was centered on the festival of Mictecacihuati, which was celebrated in various forms and under various names by the ancient Olmec, Mixtec, and Tarascan peoples. Mictecacihuati was the wife of Miclantecuhtli—a dead god who ruled over Mictlan a kind of Aztec Afterlife that was supposed to lie somewhere in the north.

From here they might watch the events that went on in their own communities, but might not really intervene in them. However, on one day—the feast day of Mictecacihuati—they were allowed to enter the world of the living and participate in the festivities. Mictecacihuati herself presided over these revels and was named the Lady of Death or the Lady of the Bones. She had the power to bring cadavers back to life and animate them for a day, at the end of which her power waned and the dead returned to their graves. In some cases, she is known as Santa Muerte—St. Death—and is portrayed as a kind of Grim Reaper with an hourglass and a scythe, although the Christian church has always disputed the name and the image.

In some parts of Mexico, the Festival is split into two broad sections. The first, on the November Ist, is known as El Dia de los Angelitos (The Day of the Little Angels), and on this day only the cadavers of small children return from the tomb. At this time, they interact with parents, relatives, and former friends, and are given sweetmeats, usually in the form of sugar skulls. The second part of the Festival (usually held on November 2nd) is known as El Dia de Los Defundos (the actual Day of the Dead) when all others who have died return—some reputedly as skeletons—in order to acknowledge Our Lady of the Bones.

Even though this is a grim time when graves open, the dead are treated like honored guests, and there is much gaiety at their return. With the accent on merriment, tequila, mescal, and pulque are consumed in large quantities to add to the festivities, and *calavaras de azucar* (sugar skulls) are handed out to young children. Indeed the whole day takes on a carnival atmosphere with people dressed in bizarre clothing and calavaras (skull masks). Many pretend to be the returning dead, and many woman are adorned in skull masks moving grandly about in the style of a *catrina.* This is the female equivalent of the Spanish *catrin* or dandy, which is based on a painting entitled *La Calavera de la Catrina* drawn in 1913 by artist Jose Guadalupe Pasada. This painting depicts a more humorous side to Death and the walking dead. Many carry an orange marigold, which is traditionally believed to be a flower that can summon the dead.

In order to amuse the dead when they return, specially composed poems—also referred to as *calavaros*—are composed. Most of these are about death, but with a humorous slant, and their main function is to "put the dead in a good mood," so that they will not commit any form of violence against the living. The dead are also shown specially drawn pictures, usually of skeletons dressed very grandly or in humorous poses, in order to lighten their mood. The whole festival is one of frivolity and, with its roots firmly in antiquity, is seen as a mechanism for dealing with the belief in the returning revenants. Throughout the world, the Mexican Day of the Dead is well known, and is seen as a great fiesta of celebration and fun.

Northern Traditions

However, in the Baltic States far to the North, where the belief in the returning dead is also very strong, the situation is a little different than the gay festivities of the Mexican tradition. As in Mexico, the dead are thought to return from their graves at a specific time of year. In Estonia, for example, there are four designated periods during which they may return: Michaelmas (September 29th); Martinmas (November 10th); St. Catherine's Day (November 25th); and Christmas Day (December 25th). In some cases, the dead frequently wander the roads in the period between Martinmas (traditionally a significant time within the Celtic calendar as well) and St. Catherine's Day, and are known as *kodukaija* (wanderers). These are not ghosts, but corporeal beings (as opposed to *vele* meaning spirit or shadow) that can sometimes do harm to those who they meet.

In Lithuania, these wandering dead are particularly aggressive and can spread disease among communities. Some blame the dead for the great epidemic in the country during the years 1710–1711, which decimated a third of the Lithuanian population. In ancient Lithuania and in the Estonian southeast, which is a stronghold of the Setus peoples, the "patron" of these revenants is the goddess Giltine, who is generally regarded as the Goddess of Death. She roughly corresponds to the Mexican Santa Muerto, Our Lady of the Bones, in appearance. She carries a scythe and is dressed in black. However, in other part of Lithuania, she is dressed completely in white, sometimes with the face of a skull. In some depictions she has a lolling spiked tongue, in some ways similar to the Indian goddess Kali, which contains poisons and diseases of various sorts. In some parts of southern Lithuania, she takes the form of an owl. She has the power of life and death, and it is she who grants the cadavers permission to return to the world of the living.

Again, as in Mexico, when the dead return from their graves, they are to be welcomed and placated by the living. If this is not done then misfortune and disease will surely follow. It was an old Setus belief that, for six weeks after death, the cadaver of the dead person lingers close to his or her former house during which time it had to be cared for, fed, entertained, and so on, by members of its own family. There is an old Baltic proverb that may have originated from the Tarvashu region of southeastern Estonia: "Whose souls are hungry, their fields are empty," meaning that, if they are not placated, the walking dead will inevitably bring disease and famine in their wake. In Lithuania, belief in the walking dead seems to have been at its strongest in the late 14th century. This was probably because in 1387, after marrying a Polish princess, the Grand Duke Jogaila issued a decree that all religions and beliefs were to be tolerated, including many Pagan ideas.

Later, the Lutheran Church clamped down strongly on such traditions and forbade them. However, the belief in the walking dead still flourished in the more rural areas of the countryside. In some areas, however, the beliefs were incorporated into the standard Christian ideas surrounding All Saints/All Soul's Day and Halloween. On November 1st, it was said that the dead returned to their former homes to ask their relatives to pray for them and to pay the local minister for offering up formal prayers on their behalf. This, of course, kept local clergymen supplied with money at a time that was probably pretty meager.

In some respects, the *kodukaija* resembled the Scandinavian *draugr*. Both would not rest in their graves—although the former only appeared at certain times of the year—and both could turn violent, particularly toward their own families, if provoked. Indeed, on certain nights of the year both Estonians and Lithuanians stayed within their houses after dark and would not venture out, for fear of meeting the walking dead on the roads and inadvertently offending them.

China's Beliefs

In China, ghosts and revenants were feared and placated in similar ways, and there were similar attempts at avoiding them when they returned from the grave. In fact the great Chinese philosopher Confucius stressed the importance of "respecting gods and ghosts, but staying away from them." Many Chinese "ghosts" were considered to be corporeal and seemed vastly hostile toward the living. As in many other cultures, the dead needed to be placated. Consequently there were numerous ghost festivals reflecting various strands of Chinese belief.

The two most famous of these were the Chinese Ghost Festival, which traced its roots back into ancestral Taoist antiquity, and the Ullambana or Deliverance Festival, which was more influenced by the Buddhist tradition and belief. These occurred during the 15th day of the seventh lunar month (known as the Ghost Month)—roughly about halfway through the year—in what was known in Western terms as Half July. During this time, it was believed that the Good Brethren—those who had been buried in accordance with proper rites and had therefore not consorted with demons—returned from the Lower Realms to spend some time with their families. Some of these were not even in human shape, but might take a variety of guises such as birds, cats, or creeping things, whereas some took bizarre and fantastic forms.

Even some of the human-looking dead had, similar to Japanese ghosts, no feet and sometimes no legs. At this time, Taoist and Buddhist priests could absolve the dead of their sufferings and inconveniences in the Afterlife through various prayers and rituals. Sometimes, it was believed, the guilty dead, or those who had committed crimes or social offenses, or who had not been buried properly, might return to be forgiven and absolved. A similar festival in Vietnam was known as the *Tet Trung Nguyen*, which was the Vietnamese equivalent of the Ullambana. This also involved honoring the dead and sweeping out their tombs in order to placate them, so that they would not return to the world among great havoc. Sometimes there were also processions—a kind of ghost cavalcade—that often had overtones of the Mexican El Dia de los Muertos. This version of the feast was also celebrated in the Chinese New Territories (Hong Kong) and took the form of a public holiday.

Sometimes more vengeful cadavers might emerge from their tombs during the Ghost Month. These hostile ancestors took physical shape and could be incredibly violent. Therefore, they needed to be distracted and placated. Their festival was known as Yue Laan (the Festival of the Hungry Ghosts). This was usually held in August or September and was once again held in the New Territories. It was a time when the restless and angry dead paraded along the streets of the remote villages, seeking out living humans to torment as they went. The local populace often tried to distract them by keeping to their houses, but leaving offerings of food on the steps to feed the passing ghosts and cadavers. Along the roadsides people could (and still can) be seen leaving offerings of fruit and flowers or burning counterfeit money as further offerings to the walking dead, in the hope that the revenants would pass them by and leave them alone. In Hong Kong itself, the festival would grow to a fairly major event, which could then be used as a tourist attraction for the city.

Preta

Since these hungry ghosts (the corporeal walking dead) feature in a number of Eastern cultures, a further word needs to be said about them and the origins of their festival. Taoists believe that certain people—for one reason or another—cannot find that which they desire in the Afterlife. They cannot, for example, fulfill their basic needs of shelter, food, or comfort, and so they return to the world of the living in order to enjoy them. However, their sustenance is slightly different from the food that mortals enjoy—it is said to be based on the emotions that the returning dead find around them.

Consequently, they attempted to scare those who they meet, or violate the houses that they passed in order to live off the fear or anxiety of mortals similar to vampires. In Tibet such creatures are known as preta (a Sanskrit word), and are counted as corporeal in order to distinguish them from the *tulpa* (often violent but unseen spirits—a bit like poltergeists) in Tibetan ghostlore. The word *preta* is derived from two Sanskrit words *pra* and *ita*, which literally means "one who departs" or "the deceased," and referred to all dead. However, it has come to mean violent and corporeal revenants that have become this way, according to Buddhist teaching, because of bad *karma*. Both Tibetans and Taoist Chinese believe that it is the shape or configuration of the house that attracts the walking dead to it and to the family within. The walking dead can, however, be driven away by a series of rituals performed by a Taoist or Buddhist priest. Indeed, part of this early philosophy has been incorporated into Buddhist thinking and, for Buddhists, the Hungry Ghost is sometimes counted as one of the stages of reincarnation.

In Buddhist tradition, the notion of the returning dead comes in part from the legend of Mahamudgalyayana, the great arhat (spiritual practitioner) who was a close follower of Shakyamuni (Siddhartha Guatama—the Buddha). Of all the Buddha's disciples, Mahamudgalyayana was the most accomplished in miracles and wonder-working. However, as a result of this, his mother was reborn into a lower realm after she had died, and was subject to great inconveniences and torments. She had been born into the realm of Hungry Ghosts because, while offering solace and advice to young monks, she had deliberately withheld money and alms from them; thus, she was condemned to the darkness with a throat so thin that she could not eat food.

Despite all his powers and his relations with ghosts and demons, the son was unable to free her from such a place, possibly because of her former behavior. The disciple approached the great Buddha about how he might free her, and the teacher advised him that she could still be brought back to the realm of the living, but that the process would be an arduous one. He was to take some food and tear it to shreds in order to draw the hungry ghost of his mother from the tomb. However, he was also to perform a ritual over each piece of food before throwing it upon clean ground for the Hungry Ghost to eat. If he would also give alms to five hundred bhikku (fully ordained Buddhist monks), then his mother would return to the world of the living. Mahamudgalyayana did all that the Buddha had instructed and his mother returned to the world of the living, although whether she was reborn or actually returned from the grave is unclear.

However, there was much celebration, and the time of her return became known as the Day of Deliverance, which forms the basis for the Buddhist Ghost Festival or Ullambana. In celebration of Mahamudgalyayana's mother's return, many other dead were supposed to return to seek absolution from the priests for their bad karma when alive. Gradually the two festivals—the Buddhist and ancient Taoist drifted closer together and finally merged into one. Some Chinese argue that there is still a difference between the two celebrations, pointing to the burning of joss sticks by the Taoists—and other

minor ritualistic niceties, but in most respects there is little to distinguish one from the other.

Japan

A variation of the festival may even be found in Japan, where it is known as *Chugen*, and is held on the July 15th. This festival is associated with Daosim (a Japanese variant of Chinese Taosim) and is primarily concerned with honoring ancestors in case they return and do some form of harm to the living. In fact, many of the rituals performed by the Japanese at this time parallel those that are carried out in China. Counterfeit money specially prepared for the purpose, for example, is burned at roadside shrines, and gifts of flowers and fruit are left at the doors of houses. This may be in case the walking dead should pass by.

There are even more curiosities connected with death and dying in Japan. These are the mysterious "living mummies" of the Mount Gassan region in Northern Japan, and particularly a famous one centred on Mount Yudono. As had already been noted, for some peoples the boundary between life and death is a very tenuous one, and the "living mummies," particularly those of the Churenji monastery on the slopes of Yudono, are ample proof of such uncertainty.

For some Buddhist ascetics, the privations of the monastic lifestyle were not nearly rigorous enough. Similar to many Christian mystics of old, they strove to demonstrate their holiness in rather severe and spectacular ways. Thus many sat, lost in religious contemplation, in the middle of deep mountain snows or in freezing torrents, or sought inaccessible and often dangerous places in order to perform their meditations. And of course, abstinence regarding food and sustenance—even abstinence to death—was often part of their regime. However, for the *true* ascetic, simply to starve oneself to death would imply too much of an interest in the physical world, and would be a positive action (that is, the taking of life) within the physical sphere. Another, more spiritual way had to be found, and the gradual creation of the "living mummy" (which took approximately more than 3,000 days to complete) fulfilled that premise. The idea of the "mummy" sprang from the teachings of the monk Kuukai, who was a prominent abbot at the temple complex on Mount Koya in northern Japan (he had studied in China for a good number of years beforehand) and was the founder of the Shingon form of Japanese Buddhism, which flourished during the Heian Period (794–1185) of Japanese history.

Living Mummies

The "living mummies" created in the remote Japanese monasteries were nothing like those that had come out of ancient Egypt, nor were they created by the same process. The Japanese "mummification" was much slower, was much more controlled, and began when the subject was alive. Generally speaking, it involved three stages.

The first stage involved a change in diet. The ascetic was to refrain from all wheat, flour, or milk products, and was only to subsist on seeds and nuts that grew within the immediate vicinity of his temple or hermitage. Further, his water intake was to decrease and he was to limit himself to a cupful every two or three days. The effect of this was to reduce his bodyweight and to draw off all the moisture that could cause fat. In this way all the extraneous tissue that would be subject to decay after death fell away. The diet also had the effect of dehydrating the ascetic's body, making it less likely to corrupt after death. This phase was to last a little more than 1,000 days (slightly more than three years).

With the second stage, the diet became much more restrictive. The ascetic was to stop taking in water completely, and was only permitted to eat the needles and seeds of the *mokijuki*, or pine trees. However, once every four or five days, he was permitted to drink a special tea made from the bark of the *urushi* tree. This tree bark is used in the preparation of ornamental lacquers and in the treatment of furniture, and is considered to be extremely poisonous to humans if ingested in large quantities. However, the ascetics only took small cups of it, throughout a matter of days, so that the toxins entering the body were miniscule. Even so, the poisons produced vomiting, intense sweating, and involuntary urination, thus dehydrating the body even further. As the toxins built up in the body, they began to kill off the parasites, maggots, and insects, which contributed to the overall decay of the bodily tissues. This process lasted for another thousand days.

By now the ascetic was little more than a skeleton, and looked like one of the walking dead himself. He was, in all probability, unable to move very far, and so it was now time for the third part of the process to begin. The monk found himself a spot where he could be walled up and more or less buried alive. The place was to be no wider than the ascetic himself, in which he could comfortably sit in the Lotus position. A gap was to be left in the stonework of the cell to enable him to breathe, and a bell was attached to the front of it. This bell was rung once each day by the ascetic to reassure his followers or bother monks that he was still alive. When the bell stopped tolling the monk was formally dead, and this was counted to be at the end of another thousand days, although the length of this stage often varied. When the holy man had died, his body was removed from the cell—usually it was little more than simply a bag of bones—and was treated with special lacquers, clothed in ceremonial robes, and placed in a shrine to be revered in the years to come.

The desiccated "mummy" was from time to time placed on display, and was supposed to have great and miraculous powers.

The most famous of all such "mummies" was perhaps that of the monk Tetsumonkai, which is still held by the Churenji Temple at Mount Yudono. It was believed that through the skull-like polished head, the spirit of the holy man could speak, utter curses, and give advice to those who came to worship there. In this aspect, the monk was still "alive" and was still interacting with the world. Until very recently, according to Sato Eimei, who was head monk at Churenji, the "mummy" of Tetsumonkai drew all sorts of ghosts and phantoms to the monastery, making is a holy and highly unusual place.

It has been estimated that in northern Japan there are between 16 and 24 of these "living mummies" still intact, and they are held in a number of remote, rural monasteries. In the late 19th century, the process of self-mummification was outlawed by the Japanese government as an illegal form of suicide. Yet, for many ascetics it was still a way of withdrawing from the material world that was in keeping with Buddhist tradition. And it was also considered to be a way of gaining further enlightenment and self-knowledge free from physical encumbrances. It is also noteworthy that many of those who began the process were old and possibly near the end of their days in any case—few young monks sought after enlightenment in this way.

The idea of the "living mummies" added a new uncertainty to death. Death was not a single event in the life of the ascetic; rather it was a gradual process of crossing over from one type of existence into the other. And because it was done throughout a long period, the process was not formally viewed as "dying," but rather as a progression toward enlightenment. The monk thus actually came to be seen as one of the "walking dead" as he progressed through the various stages of self-mummification. Although the process is supposedly

outlawed, there have been stories of such practices continuing among individual monks at isolated Japanese monasteries to this day. Perhaps the Japanese "walking dead" are still around!

Eastern Europe

For many people in the West, however, it is not the Far East that is most strongly associated with the walking dead, but rather Eastern Europe. The reason for this may be the numbers of vampire films and books, which depict the Balkan dead, rising from their graves in order to torment the living. But is such a picture actually true? Does it have an accurate origin in East European folklore?

As in Japanese folklore, the answer is a complex one. Although it has become fashionable to equate the walking dead with places such as Romania and Albania with vampirism, this is not strictly true. Not *all* East European walking dead are vampires, and there is a tradition of returning revenants outside of vampiric lore.

To differentiate between the two ideas, the Romanians use two separate words: *moroi* and *strigoi*. Although many equate the former with vampirism, this is not the case. The moroi (the plural is moroii) are simply those dead who have returned from the tomb for a specific purpose—in order to see family or to complete an unfinished task, for example. Some, it is believed, may even return in order to correct the faults of their descendants or to discipline naughty children. They are usually harmless and are often welcomed by the families whom they visit. Similar to the Western Roman Church, the Eastern Orthodox believed that there were days set aside for the returning dead who came back under a special dispensation from God or the saints.

The Strigoi

In the Orthodox Calendar there were a number of nights when the dead supposedly walked the earth. As in Lithuania, St. Martin's Eve (November 10th) was one such time, but notable too was the night of St. Sylvester's Day (Christmas Eve). Sometimes the period that lay between these two dates was a time when the dead might randomly return. But the most significant night of the year for the returning cadavers was St. George's Eve. This might fall on a number of nights—the most frequent being April 23rd (the date when most Churches—both Roman and Orthodox—agreed that the saint had died in AD 303). However, if the feast day fell within Lent, as it did in 2008, then the festival moved to Easter Monday. St. George's Eve was a designated time for the dead to return, and this was primarily the feast of the "Blessed Dead," those who had died within the proper rituals of the Church. However, one had to be wary, for the Devil, jealous of the status that God had accorded his dead servants, chose the date to release some of the more evil corpses from their tombs and allowed them to wander the countryside, creating mayhem and havoc. Romanians had to be truly careful about whom they admitted to their houses, for even their returning relatives might bring some evil intent with them.

Strigoi

The second type that characterized the walking dead was the *strigoi*. Strigoi had not died or been buried, but they had some personal characteristics that made them anti-social—anything from a physical disfigurement to unusual sexual practices to a scolding tongue. The name is thought to have originated from the Roman word *striges*, which was used to describe demons of the night and latterly witches. It may also have its roots in the word *strix*, which in Latin folklore was used to denote a shrieking vampiric bird that only appeared at night. These corpses returned to the world of the living for maligned purposes,

and were to be avoided at all costs. It was the strigoi rather than the moroi who would eventually turn into vampires once they got the taste for human blood. Usually, they attacked livestock in an attempt to drink animal blood in order to gain nourishment and warmth, but from time to time they would attack members of their own family in a similar way.

It was on St. George's Eve that both the Blessed Dead and the strigoi emerged from their graves and took to the roads, the latter often in torn, winding sheets that they had gnawed for sustenance in the darkness of their tombs. This gave them another common nickname, particularly in German-speaking areas: shroudeaters. It was easy to see where their graves lay. On St. George's Eve, a faint blue flame burned above the graves of the evil and unquiet dead—those who had committed a crime or a terrible sin in life. In fact, the grave of a robber or a murderer was usually marked in this way on this night of the year. Somewhere between 11 p.m. and midnight, it was believed, such graves burst open and the evil cadavers burst forth to torment the living. However, it was possible—so Slavic folklore said—to restrain them in their tombs if they could be pinned there and not permitted to rise. Once pinioned in the earth, the walking dead could no longer rise and cause mischief in their communities. The pinions might be a number of wooden nails driven into the hands and feet of the cadaver in an imitation of Christ on the Cross or, perhaps more effectively, a wooden stake was driven through the body of the cadaver, thus preventing the strigoi from rising. Indeed, this might be the origins of the commonly held idea of destroying a vampire with a stake. As with the vampire kind, the only proper way to dispose of the strigoi was to burn the body completely. But of course, the grave of the walking dead had first to be identified. The faint blue flame that appeared on St. George's Eve was a good indication, but it was not always reliable.

According to Professor Harry Senn in his *Vampire and Werewolf in Romania,* certain methods were often employed by local communities in order to detect the grave of a strigoi or vampire. One of these methods involved placing a very young male child on a white horse (if the horse had any impurities in its coloring, the detection would not work) and leading him to a graveyard. In some instances the horse had to be a stallion, because in many cultures stallions were considered to be magical animals. (For example, in Ireland and Scotland, witches had no power over an individual while he or she sat on the back of such a beast.) On the way through the cemetery, the horse would stop at a particular grave (or maybe even several) that would then be thoroughly inspected by community officials and the clergy. If small holes were discovered in the soil, then it was almost certainly the grave of a strigoi and the body therein would have to be exhumed and staked.

Romanian Folklore

In some parts of Romania and in Istria, the line between the living and the dead with regard to the strigoi was extremely blurred. It was often not clear as to whether exceptionally evil people had managed to somehow cheat death and extend their ghastly lives, perhaps through the dark arts, and had achieved a kind of unwholesome immortality. To reflect this confusion, two classifications had been developed within certain regions: the strigoi (denoting a living witch) and the strigoi mort (denoting a returning cadaver, risen from the tomb). Both of these were best avoided, but it was the latter who returned at specified times of the year such as St. George's Eve, Halloween, or St. Sylvester's Day, and tried to deliberately annoy the living.

According to some variants of Romanian folklore, the walking dead are invariably ginger-haired and blue-eyed. (No matter what their natural color was when alive, the hair coloring is transmuted to ginger.) They also have two hearts, which makes the staking process slightly more difficult in the case of a vampire—one may have to use *two* stakes and not one in order to destroy it. In places such as Albania, the *strigoi* are invariably of Turkish origin and resemble Turkish people. This, of course, stems from a racial antipathy between the Albanians and the Turks. In all cases, there seems to be a firm connection between the walking dead and the Romanian *pricolici*, or werewolves, and it is alleged that some of the dead have a taste for the flesh of the living, although such a belief is not universal in Romanian communities.

In some versions of old Magyar tales, there are sometimes references to certain stones, which are specialist sites at which black magicians can sometimes raise the dead. In some cases these rocks are described as "black stones," the color symbolizing the evil intent of the magicians who use them. It is this belief that supposedly influenced the famous 1931 short story by the American fantasy writer Robert E. Howard entitled "The Black Stone" and published in the magazine *Weird Tales* in November of that year. In this, Howard describes a strange monolith upon which old gods sometimes appear. They were places where the world of the living and the dead met, and some supernatural entities might cross over from one world into the other.

The black stone in Magyar stories, however, state that these may be sites where the walking dead gather in order to plot mischief against the living. However, the myth may be based on a real black stone—the al-Hajar-ul-Aswad—which is a facet of Islamic religion. This stone, according to Muslim tradition, has existed since before the time of Adam and Eve, and fell from Heaven into the world. It is still to be found in the center of the Masjid al-Haran in Mecca in Saudi Arabia, and is often a focus for many pilgrims to the city. Initially, the stone was said to have been white, but has turned black

The Black Stone

because it has absorbed so much sin and evil from the world around it. Although this particular stone has nothing to do with the walking dead it may have inspired tales of other stones that reputedly were among the Magyars, who learned of the black stone through their contact with Islamic traders. Such stones, said the East Europeans, drew the walking dead to them and could be used by people of evil intent, who knew the proper rituals to bend such cadavers to their will.

Polish Mythology

Some notion of the dead gathering at special sites at certain times of the year also appears in Polish mythology. Here, the sites are not designated by black stones, but by shrines to Zwyie, the goddess of death and rebirth. Zwyie, whose emblem is the cuckoo, is probably the representation of an old fertility god; there are legends concerning her that are similar to both Greek and Roman mythologies concerning goddesses who descended into the Underworld for a time. She conquers death and returns to the world of the living just in time for spring, and brings her retinue of the recently dead with her. They gather around her shrines, accosting those who pass by for food and drink before they return to the grave. From these points they wander abroad, sometimes visiting their former homes and sometimes creating mischief in the countryside. Zwyie is certainly the embodiment of an old pre-Christian Polish spirit, and may well have one time been one of the chief goddesses of the Elbe Slavs. She also sometimes contains certain elements of another pre-Christian deity: Zwelzda Polnoca, one of the three Zoryas of ancient Polish lore. The Zoryas were three crones who guarded the Universe and were in charge of the cycles of death and rebirth, which kept it stable. Zwelzda Polnoca was the goddess who was charged with death and rebirth—it was to her arms that the sun came to die at the end of each day, and from which it rose the following morning. Thus, similar to Zwyie, she had the power of life and death, and was able to call the dead from their graves in order to do her bidding. Throughout the years, the notion of the crone and Zwyie have become entangled and more firmly linked to the recall of the dead.

Tales of the Dead

But it was not only on Halloween (October 31st) that the *marbh bheo* might return. Indeed on May Eve (April 30th) and Martinmas (October 10th) they might also come back. And when they did, they behaved very much in the style of living—they ate, drank, smoked a pipe, played cards or other games of chance, and even enjoyed conjugal rights with their former partners. And in some of the more remote areas—particularly in Ireland—there were tales of marriages between the living and the dead. The idea (which was relatively common in Ireland around the 18th and 19th centuries) forms the basis of the ghostly short story "Schalken the Painter" (or more properly "A Strange Event in the Life of Schalken the Painter") by Irish writer Joseph Sheridan Le Fanu (1814–73).

Although the story is set in Holland and involves truly Dutch historical figures, the basis for the tale is unquestionably Irish, a fact that Le Fanu himself hints at as he states that it comes from the private papers of the Reverend Francis Purcell P.P. of Drumcoolagh in Ireland. The two protagonists in the tale, the master painter Gerrit Dou and his pupil Gottfrid Schalken (Schaleken) are both actual figures. Dou (1613–1675) was a master of one of the Flemish schools of painting based at Leyden in Holland, whereas Schalken (born 1643) was his pupil for a time. According to the story, Dou was also the guardian of his niece Rosa, with whom Schalken was secretly in love. However, being penniless at the time, he could not afford to ask Dou for her hand in marriage, and the painter, anxious to find a good marriage for his ward, married her off to the mysterious Wilken Vanderhousen of Rotterdam. Vanderhousen passed himself off as an old man, but in the end was revealed to be an animated corpse who took Rosa back with him to his tomb and beyond Schalken's reach. In despair, the pupil painted one of his finest pictures—*Girl with a Candle*—and this too is an actual portrait, painted by Gottfried Schalken, which can be seen today, hanging in the Galaria Pitti in Florence. It has been suggested that seeing this portrait inspired Le Fanu to write the tale. The actuality of the characters and of the painting brings a mysterious and rather sinister element to the tale. Did the events recounted in the tale *really* happen in early modern Holland? Obviously Le Fanu wanted us to think so.

The story, however, is probably based on an old country folktale from the south Armagh/County Monaghan border country. The story itself is said to be of great antiquity, and Le Fanu may have heard it or one similar to it. The story is known as "Grainne Daly's Wedding" and it tells of how the rather unprepossessing Grainne, who lives in abject poverty with her widowed mother, tries to find a good match for herself and finally married Thady Walsh of Killycard in County Monaghan who, it transpires, has been dead for some time, but returned to the world of the living. He takes her back with her to his tomb in a ruined church at Muckno where they are attended by other long-dead cadavers from his dark family. Variants of this tale are to be found in the more remote parts of Ireland and also in some parts of Scotland; the idea of the living marrying the dead is therefore not unusual in Celtic lore.

There are also stories of brides or bridegrooms who were somehow killed on the way to the wedding, but nevertheless continued on their journey and made their way to the ceremony and took their wedding vows before either collapsing as a rotting corpse or else vanishing away altogether. In this case, it was the will and desire to be married, which, many argued, had transformed them into the walking dead. Often they were accompanied by spectral phenomena such as ghostly carriages, which often conveyed them to the ceremony and later spirited them and their partners away into the Afterlife.

But it was not only those who wished to marry who returned to the world of the living in corporeal form. There was an old Irish saying: "A man who dies owing money or a woman who leaves a newborn child will never rest quiet in the grave." Nursing mothers in particular (those who had died when giving birth) were often permitted to return from beyond death in order to suckle their offspring in the crib. Sometimes, the fact that a corpse had returned from the grave could confer great gifts on the child that the cadaver attended. Again, on a personal note, around the age of 12, I was taken by my grandmother to see a local wise woman who reputedly had a cure for the ringworm from which I was suffering at the time. The "cure," which this woman possessed, had been acquired in a special way. Her mother had died in giving birth to her and her father had raised her. However, each night the mother had returned from the grave in order to suckle her, and in doing so had conferred the "cure" on her. There was a downside to this gift, though: For the greater part of her life she was known as "The Corpse's Daughter," and no man would even consider marrying her, as they were just too frightened of her imagined powers.

Again, the cadaver of a debtor might also return in order to complete some task that could absolve him or her of the debt, or else return in order to complete work that they had solemnly promised to do. Thus, workmen might return from the tomb (with God's permission, of course) in order to cut corn or to repair walls, while maids might return to milk cows, churn butter, or bake bread or cakes. As soon as the task was complete or the debt paid, they would return to their graves permanently and for eternity. Apart from Ireland, such traditions were held in parts of England, Wales, Scotland, and the Isle of Man and in Brittany as well—indeed all across the Celtic world.

The Corpse's Daughter

Arab Cultures

It has already been noted how voodoo bokors and mambos in West Africa and Haiti were reputedly able to raise the dead for their own end. However, the voodoo practitioners were not the only ones who could allegedly raise cadavers by their magic and for their own ends. The roots of summoning the dead in corporeal form stretch far back into antiquity, and are often seen among the nomadic tribes of the Arabian deserts. Although many of these tribes in such places as southern Jordan are mainly Muslim, evidence of pre-Islamic beliefs still survive. These are maintained by shamans who are called *fugara*; they have links into the spirit world, and can summon ghosts and demons in whatever form they wish. Sometimes this is done through spirit possession and sometimes it is through a body or physical construct (a doll or image), which will house the entity. The name *fugara* is a Bedouin word meaning "weak"—simply because the practitioner abstains from large meals and practices abstinence in order to increase his magical powers. This leaves him both skinny and weak. Much of the *fugara's* work is concerned with healing and warding off spirits, but occasionally he is called upon to bring back the dead. As in basic voodoo, much of Bedouin belief dictates that events in the world are determined by three types of entities: ancestors, the gods, and the djinn (spirits). Those who could command any of these would have mastery over the world and perhaps even over life and death. The *fugara*, who could recall the dead—whether corporeally or by spirit possession—was considered to be extremely powerful indeed. The raising of the dead was achieved through calling back, through elaborate ritual, the ancestors of those who had gone before or by calling on the djinn who dwelt in the empty deserts wastes. These spirits might revive the dead and bring them back in the form of *guul*, which has been Anglicised into the word *ghoul.* Originally the guul were a form of angel or demon that might possess and animate the bodies of the dead, usually for evil purposes. Indeed the distant star Algol (the demon star) takes its name from the ancient Arabic astronomers who named it *Al Guul* (or *Rhas-al-Guul*—the head of the demon), and it was declared to be a force that controlled the dead. The guul were said to inhabit underground dwellings, which were indistinguishable from traditional graves, from which they emerged at night in order to do harm to the living. These were bodies, it was said, that were occupied by dark spirits and were extremely dangerous. Over time, the notion of the ghoul seems to have become more defined, and it emerged as an evil spirit that fed on the corpses of the dead, which it unearthed from their graves. However, these beings might be called from the earth and controlled by a *fugara* through magical incantations, and might even be used to do mischief in a community.

Similar to the Magyar, the Bedouins believed that there were places in the world where the realm of spirits and ghosts crossed into our own. Such a place was the Rub-al-Khali or the Empty Quarter—a vast desert on the Arabian Gulf. The name Rub-al-Khali means "one with the wind," and it is one of largest areas of continuous sand in the world. According to the lore of a type of Bedouin shaman known as the *muqarribun* or Ghost Priests, there is a deeper, hidden significance to the name. This is an entrance to another world from which the djinn and the corporeal dead travel into the world of the living, being given as a "secret door to the Void that lies beyond all things." From this region, it was believed, the bodies of the dead, driven by an evil intent, wandered out into the wider world. The Ghost Priests, nevertheless, claimed they could control these walking cadavers and protect certain communities from harm.

Another place, sacred to the Bedouins and the *muqarribun*, lies in the deserts of present-day southern Jordan. This is Wadi Rum, a deep valley cut into the sandstone and granite of the area, which is something of a major tourist attraction today. The word *rum* is taken to mean "elevated," and many scientists take the original Arabic pronunciation of the name, which is *Raam*. Similar to the Rub-al-Kahali, Wadi Rum is another of these crossing places for the djinn and the Arab walking dead. It contains a number of rather spectacular rock formations that were the inspiration for T.E. Lawrence's book

Wadi Rum

Seven Pillars of Wisdom. The *muqarribun* claim that some of the rock formations within the wadi are all that remains of an ancient city, built by the djinn and populated by the dead. This legend is thought to have been the inspiration for the American horror writer H.P. Lovercraft's *Irem of the Pillars.* In this area, the dead are still supposed to dwell, manifesting themselves at night, their presence only registered by jackal-like calls.

Nabatean Civilization

The idea of the returning dead around the mysterious Wadi Rum may arise from the vanished and enigmatic Nabatean civilization, which flourished in the region in Roman times. Perhaps it is because an air of great mystery has attached itself to this ancient people that they have become imbued with mysterious knowledge and powers. Little is known about this early Semitic culture except that they were a trading civilization that benefited extensively from dealing with the Romans, who eventually turned on them and brought their civilization under Roman rule. A tribe of mysterious shamans known as the *Al Sulaba.* who inhabit the Arabian Peninsula, are believed to be perhaps their last descendants. These nomadic tribes are often known as the "Lost Shamans" of the Arabian Desert and are credited with a number of supernatural powers, including bringing back the dead in corporeal form. They are regarded as great healers over whom death has no control. Some anthropologists actually believe them to be of Indian origin, and others believe them to be from a pre-Islamic people who inhabited the area. Because of their extremely fair skin, some have even postulated that they might be of Crusader origin.

Little hard evidence is available concerning the Nabateans apart from the ancient and now abandoned desert capital at Petra in south Jordan, which has become a Jordanian tourist attraction. It is also believed that from Petra they controlled a prosperous trading empire that managed the crossroads between the Arabic and Western civilizations. It is thought that they traded with the Arabs, the Greeks, and the Romans, before the fall of the empire under their last king, Rabbel II, to the might of Rome around AD 106. They were then absorbed into the Pax Romana under the name of Arabia Petrea, and their culture merged with that of their conquerors. However, they were considered by some to be the custodians of arcane wisdom, which has been passed down across the centuries to the Al Sulaba.

The Bedouin muqarribun are very wary of the Al Sulaba, believing them to be in control of the deserts djinn and the dead. They are said to be somehow connected to Wadi Rum and perhaps even to the Rub-al-Khali, and to know the "secrets of the Void" (Afterlife) that are denied to others. Even today, extremely little is actually known about the "Lost Shamans," and their way of life is still highly secret. Anthropological investigators in the late 19th century, such as Sir Richard Burton and William Belgrave, visited them, but were unable to ascertain their origin—and this still remains the case today. But among Bedouins, the idea that they guard ancient wisdoms concerning the corporeal dead is still very rife. Many of the Bedouin peoples shun them, and no Bedouin man will take a wife from among their kind. Few photographs outside of those taken by 19th-/early-20th century scientists exist, and it's not really known if they still inhabit the Arabian deserts today as a distinct people. Their tradition of maintaining a "secret knowledge" handed down from the ancient Nabateans, which included the power to call forth the dead, however, has continued and still seems to be evident amongst many Bedouins today.

The lore of the fugara, the muqarribun, and the Al Sulaba have become intertwined throughout the years with notions of Wadi Rum and the Rub-al-Khali—the "secret gateways into the Void"—to create a mythology in the Arab

mind in which the dead return at specified "crossings" between their world and ours, and can be summoned by those skilled enough in the arcane arts to do so. And lurking somewhere in the background is the brooding, menacing figure of the guul, the dweller in the graveyard, and perhaps one of the most potent embodiments of the walking dead. As in other civilizations the Arabian cadavers may not be all that far away in Islamic belief, even in modern times.

The returning dead, therefore, appear in the lore and traditions of many cultures all across the world, from ancient times to the present day. Their presence signals the belief that death is not the ultimate end, and that something lies beyond. They also give an assurance that humans are immortal and that they can, if need be, return to reassure—or perhaps to comfort or advise—those whom they have left behind. They are also the last vestiges of vanished cultures and arcane beliefs, reminding subsequent generations of all that has gone before. And as such, they continue to haunt our minds—whether it be through continuing beliefs, in tales, or in celluloid form—and perhaps will do so for many years to come.

Conclusion

Figures From Beyond the Grave

There is an old Irish legend concerning the celebrated St. Columcille (with a Scottish variant where it refers to St. Columba, who is, of course, the same man). Although the tale varies, its underlying meaning is the same in both countries.

In the Irish version, the saint's follower Odhrain died and was buried. (In the Scottish version he gives himself as a sacrifice so that Columba's abbey on Iona can be built.) Columcille/Columba grieved for his friend and wished him back into the world. Gathering a number

Odhrain

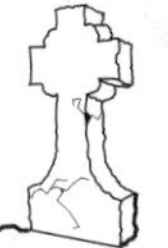

of followers at the side of Odhrain's grave, he prayed that the dead man might be restored, and God granted his wish. The earth parted and Odhrain sat up, blinking in the sunlight. Of course the saint's other followers gathered around, anxious to know what death was like, and if there was an Afterlife. Odhrain simply shrugged and replied: "Actually death is no great mystery and Hell is not nearly as bad as the Church would have us believe." Outraged and horrified at this revelation, the saint commanded Odhrain to be dead once more, and he fell back and ordered the others to cover him in clay to prevent him rising again. This gave rise to the old saying among the early Gaelic Christians—"Ur!Ur! air beul Odhrain" ("Earth! Earth! On Odhrain's mouth"), thus denying any revelation of the Afterlife or any possibility of return from the dead. The tale is taken as an attempt by the early Church to do away with surviving Pagan notions regarding death and resurrection. This wariness and prohibition hints at how deeply ideas of death, what lies beyond, and the possibility of return from the grave, lies within the human psyche.

For many ancient peoples death was the final unknown, just as it is today. Nobody knew what death actually was; was it, for instance, the end of all things and the end of an individual's involvement in the material world (as we believe it to be today), or was it simply a process by which the individual passed from one reality to the next? Furthermore, nobody actually knew for certain what lay on the other side, and if, as some ancient civilizations believed, it was merely a process of transfer from one sphere of existence to another, might that process be reversed, thus allowing the dead to return to the world of the living, albeit perhaps in a temporary capacity? Other questions abounded, too: Were the dead aware of what was going on in the living world? Could they influence affairs in that world? Were

Phantom

they supportive to their descendants, or jealous and hostile toward those who survived them? If they returned, would they do harm and would they need to be placated?

Gradually attempts to answer at least some of these questions began to coalesce into a corpus of belief and lore that surrounded the idea of returning

revenants, some of which incorporated elements of some very ancient perceptions. As the civilizations began to come together, many of these beliefs persisted on the fringes of society, taking on definite and distinctive shapes, often of a terrifying or menacing aspect—the *draugr,* the mummy, or the zombie. Many of the developing belief systems assimilated them, too, usually depicting them as night terrors or dark creatures to be avoided. In the Christian West, the Church found itself in an awkward, not to say difficult, position. Having placed a great deal of emphasis on the Afterlife and the hope of attaining Salvation from Hell, it could hardly deny the ancient notions of returning corpses, which could be taken as proof of at least part of what it taught. So it began to devise ways of explaining the revenant that climbed from its grave in order to wander the countryside, and ideas of the Blessed Dead and the Demonic Dead seemed to explain this. This gave rise to some of the earliest supernatural fables—it might be wrong to strictly call them "ghost stories" because, nowadays, we often have a rather different perception of "ghosts"—which we have in Western Europe. The returning phantoms were not the ethereal figures of much later Victorian melodrama, but rather solid, corporeal entities that could eat, drink, smoke, injure, and enjoy sexual relations. It was assumed that they could also kill.

And of course, the Christian tradition was not the only one to embrace the idea of cadavers returning from the tomb. West African, Egyptian, and Eastern cultures also mentioned such lore and had belief systems that incorporated the idea of walking revenants. And throughout the years, some of these beliefs, and the often, frightening figures that embodied them, found their way into the fringes of mainstream Westernized horror fiction and cinema—the zombie, the mummy, the ghoul, or the zuvembie—to terrify readers and viewers just as old tales concerning the walking dead had done many centuries before.

The idea of returning revenants has also been strengthened in the popular consciousness by medical conditions such as catalepsy, in which the "deceased" have not been dead at all, but in a coma-like condition, reviving after a period of time and resuming normal life. Conditions such as this may well have been more common in former times than we imagine in a period when medicine was slowly developing. And as we have noted, the idea of grave robbers—the bodysnatchers who flourished during the 18th and 19th centuries—also added to the terrifying images of rising cadavers. It was stories of graves being opened and their contents removed that presented a chilling and terrifying spectacle to the society of the time and underscored the idea that corpses might somehow rise and re-enter the world of the living. In an age when science was gaining hold these ideas and beliefs harked back to more primal fears, and to an earlier era when the walking dead might very well stalk the roads as soon as the sun went down.

Something of that same element remains in our society today. Many modern horror stories and "fright films" often include the menacing figures of returning revenants that usually terrify protagonists (and the readers or the audience) with their fearful appearance. The fear of the corpse rising from the grave still lies deep within every one of us, as does the belief that such revenants are agents of evil and will invariably mean us harm. Perhaps it is with this ancient terror nestling somewhere in our minds that many of us can echo the words of the venerable Abbe Serapion in Theophile Gautier's often neglected classic of Gothic fiction *La Morte Amoreuse:*

> *"My son, I must warn you. You are standing on with one foot raised on the brink of an abyss; take heed that you do not fall therein. Satan's claws are long and tombs are not always true to their trust."*

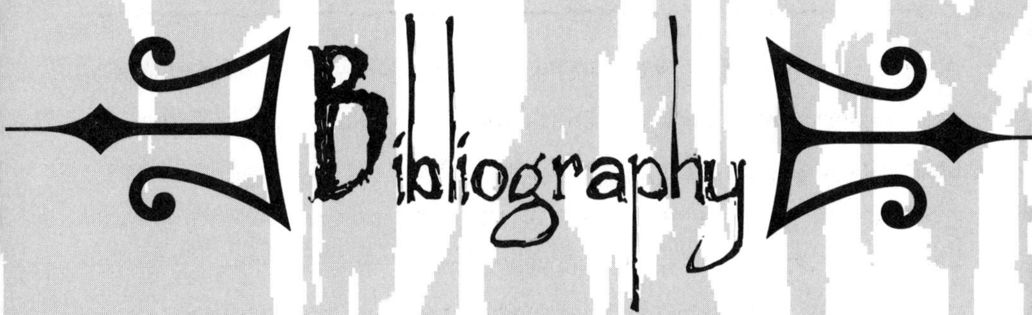

Archer, B. *Zombies: An Anthology*. Toronto: Zebra Publishing, 1965.

Arnesson, Jon. *Viking Ghosts*. Stockholm, Sweden: Stockholm Press, 1962.

Arnold, James. *The Lost Shamans*. New York: Zoroaster Press,1963.

———. *The Mystery of Wadi Rum*. New York: Zoroaster Press, 1961.

Atwater, P.M.H. *Coming Back to Life*. New York: Ballantine Books, 1991.

Barber, Paul. *Vampires, Burial and Death: Folklore and Reality*. New Haven, Conn.: Yale University Press, 1988.

Bogatyrev, Petr. *Vampires in the Carpathians—Magical Acts, Rites and Beliefs in Subcarpathian Rus*. New York: East European Monographs, 1998.

Bulfinch, Thomas. *Myths and Legends of the Dead.* Hertfordshire, Ireland: Wordsworth Press, 1988.

Byock, Jesse, ed. *The Prose Edda.* New York: Penguin Press, 2005.

Caulfield, Ann. *A Dreadful Story of Burke and Hare.* Edinburgh, Scotland: Murchison Press, 1889.

Curran, Bob. *Encyclopaedia of the Undead.* Franklin Lakes, N.J.: New Page Books, 2006.

———. *Vampires.* Franklin Lakes, N.J.: New Page Books, 2005.

Daren, Maya. *Daren Divine Horsemen: Living Gods of Haiti.* New York: McPherson Press, 1998.

D'Auria, Sue D., Peter Lacovara, and Catherine Roehring. *Mummies and Magic: The Funerary Arts of Ancient Egypt.* Dallas, Tex.: Dallas Museum of Art, 1993.

Davis, Wade. *The Serpent and the Rainbow.* New York: Pocket Editions, 1997.

El-Shamay, Hasan. *Tales Arab Women Tell.* Bloomington, Ind.: Indiana University Press, 1999.

———. *Types of Folktale in the Arab World—A Demographically Oriented Tale-Type Index.* Bloomington, Ind.: University Press, 2004.

Fanucane, Ronald C. *Ghosts: Appearances of the Dead and Cultural Transformation.* Amherst, N.Y.: Prometheus Books, 1996.

Felton, D. *Haunted Greece and Rome: Ghost Stories from Classical Antiquity.* Dallas, Tex.: University of Texas Press, 1999.

Fleetwood, Dr. John. *The Irish Bodysnatchers.* Dublin: Tomar Publishing, 1988.

Hamilton-Paterson, James. *Mummies: Life and Death in Ancient Egypt.* New York: Viking Press, 1979.

Harn, Lafcadio. *In Ghostly Japan.* New York: Charles E. Tuttle & Co., 1971.

Ikram, Salima, and Aidan Dodson. *The Mummy in Ancient Egypt: Preparing the Dead for Eternity.* New York: Thames and Hudson, 1998.

Johnston, S.I. *Restless Dead: Encounters Between the Living and the Dead in Ancient Greece.* Berkeley, Calif.: University of California Press, 1999.

Jones, Ernst. *On the Nightmare.* New York: Grove Press, 1951.

Joynes, Andrew. *Medieval Ghost Stories.* Rochester, N.Y.: Boydell Press, 2006.

Kirk, David. *Sumerian and Assyrian Legends.* New York: Dorchester Press, 1951.

Kvideland, Reimund, and Henning K. Sehmsdorf, eds. *Scandinavian Folk Belief and Legend.* Minneapolis, Minn.: University of Minnesota Press, 1988.

LeBraz, Anatole. *The Celtic Legend of the Beyond.* London: Llanerch Press, 1993.

Ledbetter, Rev. J.C. *And Death Shall Have No Dominion—A Consideration Regarding the Dead: A Believer's Guide.* Asheville, N.C.: Spiritual Publishing, 1981.

Matraux, Alfred, and Hugo Charteris. *Voodoo in Haiti.* New York: Random House, 1996.

O' Donoghue, Heather. *From Asgard to Valhalla.* London: B. Taurus & Co., 2007.

Ogden, Daniel. *Witchcraft and Ghosts in Greek and Roman Worlds: A Sourcebook.* Oxford, UK: Oxford University Press, 2002.

Ohaegbulam, Clement. *West African Folk Traditions.* Lanham, Md.: University Press of America, 1997.

Ross, Catrein. *Mysterious Japan.* Tokyo: Yen Books, 1996.

Schmit, Jean-Claude. *Ghosts in the Middle Ages; Living and the Dead in Medieval Society.* Chicago, Ill.: University of Chicago Press, 2000.

Seabrook, William B. *The Magic Island.* London: Marlow Free Press, 1999.

Senn, Harry. *The Vampire and Werewolf in Romania.* Irvington, N.Y.: Columbia University Press, 1982.

Summers, Montague. *The Vampire in Europe.* New York: University Books,1929.

———. *The Vampire: His Kith and Kin.* Irvington, N.Y.: Columbia University Press,1928.

Tachetenberg, Joshua. *Jewish Magic and Superstition.* Springfield, N.J.: Behrman's House, 1939.

Tallant, Robert. *Voodoo in New Orleans.* New York: Macmillan Publishers, 1993.

Thompson, Francis. *The Supernatural Highlands.* Edinburgh, Scotland: Luath Press, 1997.

Wood, Juliet. *The Celtic Book of Living and Dying.* New York: Duncan Baird, 2000.

Woodring, Jonathan, ed. *The Otherworld Voyage in Irish Literature and History.* Dublin: Four Courts Press, 2000.

Index

C

D

E

M

N

S

T

U

V

W

Z

About the Author

Dr. Bob Curran was born in a remote area of County Down, Northern Ireland. The area in which he grew up was rich in folklore—especially the folklore of the supernatural—and this gave him an ear for and an interest in the tales and beliefs of many people. He has worked in a number of jobs before going to University, where he took a doctorate in child psychology. Even so, his interest in folklore and folk culture was still very much to the fore, and this prompted him to write a number of books on the subject, including *Celtic Lord and Legend*; *Vampires*; and *Lost Lands, Forgotten Realms.* Having taken another degree in history, he now lectures and broadcasts on matters of historical interest, and acts as advisor to a number of influential cultural bodies in Northern Ireland. Most recently he has been working on advisory bodies regarding cultural links between Northern Ireland and the West of Scotland. He currently lives in Northern Ireland with his wife and young family.

Other books by Bob Curran

The Encyclopedia of the Undead

Wallking With the Green Man

Lost Lands, Forgotten Realms

Other Paranormal Titles from NEW PAGE BOOKS

Lore of the Ghost

The Origins of the Most Famous Ghost Stories Throughout the World

EAN 978-1-60163-024-7
$14.99

Haunted Spaces, Sacred Places

A Field Guide to Stone Circles, Crop Circles, Ancient Tombs, and Supernatural Landscapes

EAN 978-1-60163-000-1
$15.99

The Ghost files

Paranormal Encounters, Discussion, and Research From the Vaults of Ghostvillage.com

EAN 978-1-56414-974-9
$13.99

Flying Saucers and Science

A Scientist Investigates the Mysteries of UFOs, Interstellar Travel, Crashes, and Government Cover-Ups

EAN 978-1-60163-011-7
$16.99

Captured! The Betty and Barney Hill UFO Experience

The True Story of the World's First Documented Alien Abduction

EAN 978-1-56414-971-8
$16.99

Witness to Roswell

Unmasking the 60-Year-Cover-Up

EAN 978-1-56414-943-7
$15.99

A Division of Career Press
NewPageBooks.com

Available Wherever Books Are Sold or Call 201-848-0310